ACADEMIC AND BUSINESS LETTERS AND EMAILS
FROM:A
TO:Z

Part I

Academic Recommendation * Acknowledgment * Adjustment
Application * Complaint * Cover * Follow-Up

By EssayShark

Table of Contents

Introduction

The art of writing letters has always been appreciated and honored. Heck, people can even fall in love through correspondence! Though the premise is questionable, it illustrates how powerful a well-tailored letter can be.

With this book you will be able to solve your educational and employment problems with one elaborate, yet concise piece of writing. A good letter is short, but packed with information, and we will teach you how to achieve this balance in your own correspondence. To create a striking piece of writing, you don't have to know anything about writing letters — just choose the category (business or academic), pick the specific type you need out of the 7 types that are analyzed (academic recommendation, acknowledgement, adjustment, application, complaint, cover, follow-up letters) and follow the guide.

Each guide is divided into five parts, leading you closer to a heart-winning letter. To ensure success, we have included two quality sample letters for each type of writing. There is no way you can escape writing letters, so it's better to master the art now, and have a good assistant around in case of an emergency. Let's say you need to handle a difficult client, respond to a complaint letter, or email a partner who seems to be avoiding all direct answers. Just find the required letter format in our book, and boom! You have a full guide and perfect template to follow. We may not teach you to love writing letters, but we definitely can teach you to write great ones.

Note About Letters and Emails

All the recommendations and instructions that you'll find in the book concern both mail and email. Samples that are created for each type of letter also fit for mailing and emailing. Despite the fact that you'll see envelopes with addresses written there, the body of the letter is absolutely suitable for emails. Though most people in the 21st century use email instead of mail, some types of letters, such as invitation letters, need to be sent by mail. For this reason, we decided to present how envelopes should be signed.

If you need to complete an email, you should just ignore the envelope and pay more attention to the letter itself. When you are writing emails, you just need to specify the email address of the recipient and the subject of the letter. The subject is usually the type of your letter and your full name separated by a period. Thus, when you need to send a cover letter, you should specify the subject the following way: "Cover letter. [Your Full Name]"

Academic Recommendation Letter Writing Guide

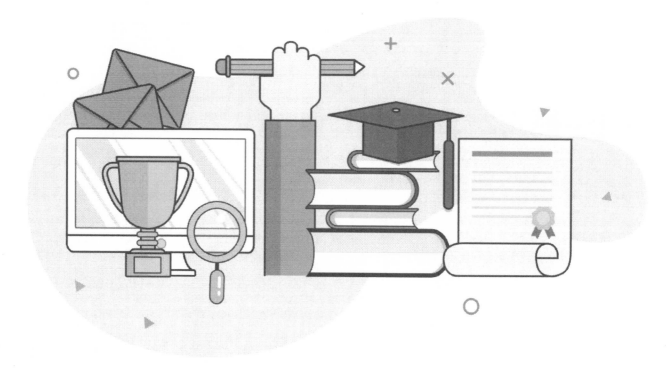

Definition and Aim of an Academic Letter of Recommendation

An academic letter of recommendation, or letter of reference, is a letter written by an educator in which they provide an assessment of the characteristics, skills, and qualifications of the student in order to support their application.

Typically, these letters are used to determine whether the person in question is suitable for a particular position — for example, for enrolling in a graduate school or program, or for obtaining a scholarship. Therefore, the major purpose of the letter is to highlight the skills, character traits, and qualifications which might be necessary for this particular position. Consequently, you as a referee must be well acquainted both with the candidate and with the institution or program he or she is applying for.

Taking into account the fact that writing recommendations for most schools and programs is a seasonal occasion, and it is possible that many students will ask for the letter simultaneously, you might consider creating a template with the key points you would be covering. This way, you would still control the process of writing, instead of letting the students write a recommendation for themselves and just signing it afterward, but would not waste too much time on it.

Remember that in this letter you provide, first and foremost, the support for the person you are writing for, so this is not a good place for excessive criticism, even if it is warranted.

A letter of recommendation is significant, and sometimes plays a decisive part of the application process. Before agreeing to write it, make sure you know the person you would be writing for, at least so you wouldn't need to make up the whole thing. Verify that the candidate is ready to provide all information you might need. Keep in mind that your letter might determine the future educational or career perspectives of your candidate, so you should approach the task with great care and responsibility. If you do not have the time or simply do not know the person in question well enough, it is better to decline their request to allow them sufficient time to look for someone who would be up to the task.

Steps on How to Write an Academic Letter of Recommendation

For writing this type of letter, collecting information is as vital as writing itself. So, to create a truly strong reference, you would need, first of all, to gather information, and then to use it in order to present your candidate in the best light possible while being honest. Here are the steps you might follow:

1. Gather as much information as possible about the person you are writing a recommendation for.

2. Set up a meeting and ask them to bring their CV or resume, and all diplomas and certificates which might be relevant for their purpose. Alternatively, ask them to send you copies via email.

3. If this person has taken your course(s) and you have any related notes, copies of their essays or something to that effect, you might want to revisit them to refresh your memory.

4. You would want to either meet with the candidate in person and inquire about their plans and ambitions or ask them to elaborate on them in written form. If they have already started composing the letter of purpose or the motivation letter, request them to send it to you, even if it is only a draft.

5. Whether you communicate personally or in written form, consider creating a specific folder where all information on your candidate would be kept, at least until you sent your letter.

6. Write out the program, the scholarship, or the school they are applying for so it would be easy for you to find. You might want to look them up on the internet.

7. Discuss with your candidate what qualities or skills they would like to have highlighted in the recommendation. You are not under any obligation to comply with their requests if you believe their self-assessment is not truthful, but it might stir your thought process and save you some writing pains.

8. Make a bullet point list of all information you want to include in your letter.

9. Highlight two to four traits you would want to emphasize through your letter consistently. Keep them in mind.

10. Make brief drafts of the paragraphs, dedicated to the specific qualities or skills.

11. Write an introduction in which you talk about yourself and your professional relation to the person you are writing for. Whether they have taken one of your selective courses, you were their research advisor, or something else, this information is extremely relevant for this kind of writing.

12. You might need several drafts. Regardless of the time you spend on this letter, remember the result should be blameless.

13. If you feel there is negative or neutral information which might be of interest to the selection committee, you might add a request to be contacted for the details.

14. Sign and send!

The Structure of an Academic Letter of Recommendation

Letters of recommendation might be more personal than many other types of academic writing. However, they also follow the typical structure, which makes both reading and writing the letters of reference a bit easier.

What to Include in Your Letter

Greetings. At the very beginning of the letter, you address the person you are writing to. The greetings are commonly aligned left.

In this type of letter, you may not know the names of your respondents. However, if they are available, you might address them in this manner:

Dear Admissions Officer First Name Last Name

If the names are unknown, you might write:

Dear Selection/Admission Committee

To Whom It May Concern

Introduction. In the opening paragraph, you introduce yourself and your professional relations to the candidate. You state your name and position and the name of the student you are writing for. Then, you write since when and for how long have you known the student. If you advised the student on their research, elaborate on this. It should be clear you have had the opportunity to get acquainted with them and assess their capabilities. You would want to be as specific as possible. Here, you may also give a brief overview of what you are going to write further.

The body of the letter. The first section would normally consist of two or four paragraphs which address the candidate's professional qualities and skills, their knowledge, activities, interests, and the results of their efforts. You would discuss the student's performance in the class, their essays or any additional roles, and responsibilities they might have in their professional capacity. If they were tutoring, serving as a TA, or have undertaken any community service relevant to their application, you would mention it here. You should be specific and detailed. It must be evident that you do know the student and can assess them adequately.

In the second section, you address their characteristics, social skills, as well as relationships with peers and superiors. Keep in mind that it is not enough to just state that the student is patient or hardworking or has leadership skills; you would need to support your claims with examples.

Closing. In the final paragraph, you summarize and emphasize the major points you want to get across about the candidate. Here you might also ask to be contacted for any further information.

Sincerely/Best regards,

Your Name,

Contact information.

Useful Expressions for Writing an Academic Letter of Recommendation

There are common phrases which might come handy regardless of the person and the institution your letter is aimed for. Here is a list of common phrase examples:

Introduction

- It is a great pleasure that I am writing this letter of recommendation for (name).

- I am writing this letter to recommend (name) for admission to (name of the program) at (name of the institution).

- I am delighted to present a recommendation for (name).

- In the past _____ years, I have taught (name) in the following classes_____.

- During the time (name) was my student at the (name of the institution) they have distinguished themselves as_____.

- I came to know (name) when I was their (your position) for (name of the course).

- (Name) worked under my supervision during their research work on (topic).

The body of the letter

- I would rank (name) in the top _____ % of the students in their class/of the students that I have taught in the past _____ years.

- (Name)'s performance is ranked as far above average.

- Throughout the years of study, (name) has shown interests in _____.

- I would highly recommend (name) for the (Master/PhD) program in (subject).

- I am confident that (name) will be an excellent addition to your academic community.

Closing

- Please do not hesitate to contact me if you have any further questions.

- Contact me if you have any question pertaining (name).

- If any highlighting is of essence, please contact me at/via _____.

- If I can be of any further assistance, please do not hesitate to contact me.

Dos and Don'ts of Academic Letter of Recommendation Writing

While writing a letter of recommendation, you would want to keep in mind some useful tips and avoid common mistakes. Both categories are listed below.

Dos

- Ask student whether the program they are applying for has any specific requirements for the content or the form and follow the instructions.

- Be mindful of the deadline!

- Mention your degree and the institution you are affiliated with. Your recommendation must look credible.

- Compare the student to their peers.

- The skills or characteristics which are the most relevant for the application should be emphasized throughout the letter.

- Show not tell. If you can provide the examples and specific cases to support your claims that the student possesses particular qualities or skills, do it.

- Each paragraph should contain several sentences.

- Be as specific as possible regarding the candidate's character and skills.

- Be personal. It is your assessment of the candidate. The purpose of the letter is to provide the information which cannot be found anywhere else in the application documents.

- Remember to concentrate on the particular qualities and skills which would be relevant for their program, school, or scholarship.

- Discuss a particular aspect of the student's work: their performance in the class, the essay they have written, their contribution to the teamwork on the project, and so on.

- Be honest. You may include criticism, as over-the-top praises are viewed with understandable skepticism, but do not indulge in it.

- Be mindful of your style and formatting.

- Proofread the letter. Make sure grammar, structure, punctuation, and style are blameless.

- Remember always to support any superlative adjectives you use regarding your student with particular examples. If the student is outstanding, you need to make the selection committee believe you.

Don'ts

- Do not agree to write for the person if you don't remember them or have nothing good to say about them.

- Don't agree to write the letter if you are not sure you would create a perfectly competent piece of writing. It is better to decline the request rather than to let the candidate down with low-quality writing.

- Don't be too brief, but do not engage in empty talk either. A letter of recommendation typically should be one to two pages.

- You may offer some quantitative assessment of the student's work, such as their GPA, but avoid simply restating what can already be found in their documents.

- Avoid general phrases like "good student," "a hard-working person," and the likes. Be specific.

- Do not delay writing for the last moment.

- Avoid, when possible, distancing yourself with phrases as "to the best of my knowledge," "as far as I know," and the likes. They might be perceived as the implied criticism or at least suggest you do not really know the candidate very well.

- Avoid ambiguous adjectives: for example, the phrase "adequate qualification" suggests implied criticism of the said qualification.

- Avoid excessive praises. When there are too many "outstanding," "excellent," and "exceptional" comments regarding your student, your recommendation is not likely to be taken seriously.

Questions and Answers on Academic Recommendation Letters

There are common questions regarding the letters of reference which might arise while you are writing, so answers will be provided for them in this section.

Q: Are there any specific forms for letters of recommendation?

A: Ask your student about the requirements for the letter. For example, some scholarships or programs may have specific forms you would need to fill or requirements for sending the hard copy of the letter. If it is not specified, you are free to write as you see fit.

Q: Do I show the letter to the student before sending it?

A: As a general rule, it is your decision. Students may waive their right to see the letter once it is written, and you might wish to advise them to do so. In many cases, you would feel freer to be sincere if you know the student would not see your writings. If you want to show it, however, it is up to you and should be decided in a case by case basis.

Q: Am I allowed to include sensitive information?

A: In requesting you to write a letter of recommendation, your candidate automatically grants you permission to disclose such information as their GPA or class ranking, so you may feel free to do it.

Q: Am I allowed to criticize the student?

A: Yes, but it is advisable for you to be moderate. You might also want to provide some context which would temper your criticism. You might discuss the circumstances extenuating the student's shortcomings or emphasize that they have overcome some obstacles and improved their performance. Anyway, being truthful is vital, but criticism just for the sake of it is not a good idea in this kind of writing.

Works Cited

Bohlin, Reme. "Writing Letters of Recommendation for Students. Tips for Educators and Guidance

    Counselors." *OWL. Purdue Online Writing Lab*, 2016,

    https://owl.english.purdue.edu/owl/resource/982/02/. Accessed 10 July 2017.

Doyle, Alyson. "Academic Recommendation Letter Examples and Writing Tips." *The Balance*,

    2017, https://www.thebalance.com/academic-recommendation-letters-2062959. Accessed 10

    July 2017.

"How to Write a Letter of Recommendation." *Eduers.com*, 2009,

    http://www.eduers.com/reference/index.htm. Accessed 12 July 2017.

"How to Write an Academic Recommendation Letter." *Answershark.com*, 2017,

    https://answershark.com/writing/academic-letters/how-to-write-academic-recommendation-

    letter.html. Accessed 8 July 2017.

"Writing a Recommendation Letter." *Academic Help*, 2012, https://academichelp.net/letter-writing-

    help/write-recommendation-letter.html. Accessed 9 July 2017.

Academic Recommendation Letter for Master's in Engineering

Return Address

Michael Manning
The University of Montreal
2900 Edouard Montpetit Blvd.
Montreal, QC H3T 1J4

Recipient's Address

Roger Mills
McGill University
845 Rue Sherbrooke Ouest
Montréal, QC H3A 0G4

Dear Mr. Mills,

As the professor of Computer Engineering and Information at the University of Montreal, I thoroughly recommend Peter Herston for acceptance at your university. I have played the role of teacher and mentor to Mr. Herston during his time at our university. Having worked with him for three years, I have witnessed his scholarly feats, and feel completely confident in writing this recommendation letter.

Our academic activity was not limited exclusively to the university program, as we participated in different engineering projects together. I can say that Mr. Herston has demonstrated his professionalism since the day he came to my class. His astuteness is such that I have never had to give extra instructions for his projects. Moreover, I have felt as though I were working with a colleague instead of a student. His knowledge goes far beyond the syllabus, and has achieved great results in developing neuro-electronics projects and software.

First of all, I must say that Mr. Herston is one of the most talented students I have ever taught in my career. His mathematical and physical thinking is exceptional, as he could always solve tasks, even without the necessary tools. It is my firm belief that Peter was born to be an engineer. At our university, engineering courses are extremely hard, and exams are very difficult because we developed them not only to check the course material, but to test students' ability to think differently. That is, the main task is always to find an alternative way of solving each task. For this reason, most of our students cannot pass the exams at first try. This is what differentiates Mr. Herston from most other students. His ability to think differently has thoroughly impressed my colleagues and I. Even in the final exam last year, he scored 100 points, while 94% of students had failed the exam. There is no need to mention that he mastered programming languages (Pascal, C++, Python, Java, PHP) even before entering our university and now uses them impeccably.

It is worth mentioning that, while working on projects, Peter demonstrates innovative thinking. While most students solve the given tasks according to the textbook, Mr. Herston uses his intuition and finds more practical solutions. That is why I can certainly say that he would be an excellent candidate for a master's degree in the field of engineering in your university. Judging from his exam marks, it is evident that his proficiency in computer engineering alone is enough to apply for the master's program.

One more trait of his character I would like to emphasize is patience. Six months ago, I gave him an extraordinary task outside the curriculum, simply to check his qualities. I knew that it would take months or even years to debug the code I sent; nevertheless, it was an exciting experiment. Last week he sent me the working program with entirely clear code. I could not even imagine that anybody would put this much effort for such a task. Therefore, Mr. Herston is one of few who will finish a job no matter how much time and effort it would require.

Peter Herston is interested in many fields of computer science and engineering; however, his attention is concentrated on the development of neuro-electronics and artificial intelligence. In his course work, he proposed realistic and practical methods of how neuro-electronics technologies can boost the process of AI developments. For this work, he received the highest grade on the course because, in my opinion, a project of that level could be written only by a Master of Engineering. For this particular reason, I strongly recommend Mr. Herston for the Master's Degree in Engineering at your University.

Sincerely,

Michael Manning,
Professor of Computer Engineering and Information,
University of Montreal,
Phone number: +1-613-555-0132

Academic Recommendation Letter – International Airline Company

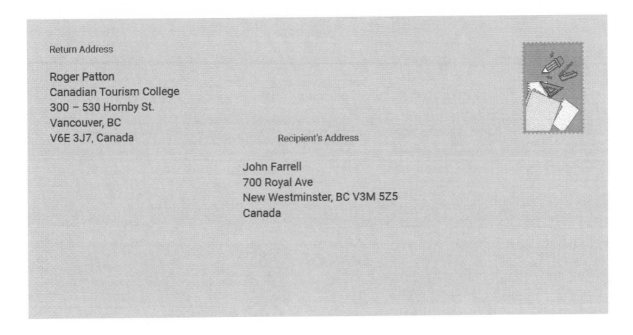

Return Address

Roger Patton
Canadian Tourism College
300 – 530 Hornby St.
Vancouver, BC
V6E 3J7, Canada

Recipient's Address

John Farrell
700 Royal Ave
New Westminster, BC V3M 5Z5
Canada

Dear Mr. Farrell,

By this letter, I am proud to recommend Jennifer Smith, who is a fourth-year student of the Canadian Tourism College. In the period from 2014 to 2017, she was my student. Our interests intersected in the field of socially useful activities conducted by teachers with our students. During our joint work, Jennifer showed herself as an outstanding person with a keen interest in everything that happens in the field of tourism, international flights, and other areas directly related. Participation in a number of international conferences in the field of international tourism held in Canada and the USA confirms Jennifer's desire to try her professional opportunities as a flight attendant.

In this sense, Jennifer is a serious and motivated person: she is erudite and versatile, and this gives me the right to class her among the best students of the college. The range of interests of Jennifer is not limited only to professional activities. Her public activity deserves particular attention: her preparation and participation in college competitions and social programs, and attracting other students to the public life of the college. Jennifer is not afraid to take responsibility for the safety of people. It is distinguished by self-confidence, the ability to solve problems quickly and the willingness to take on the task and perform it in the best way possible.

With full responsibility, I declare that from the training, Jennifer has mastered all the skills necessary for the successful performance of her duties as a flight attendant. From what is taught, these skills include boarding service and VIP-service on board, the culture of serving dishes, service etiquette, the basics of business etiquette, and the rules of modern etiquette and professional image. I am proud to say that she knows how to provide a friendly atmosphere aboard the airplane, to anticipate the questions and desires of passengers, and to demonstrate a genuine interest in the mental state of their wards. Also, she perfectly studied the design of the aircraft, so in the case of some unexpected situations (air pockets, thunderstorms), she will be able to explain to passengers the cause of the shaking of the aircraft, to calm them, without compromising the crew and the company. Also, I taught her how to use rescue equipment. She practiced emergency landing on land and water, successfully immersed passengers on a raft, evacuated through an inflatable ladder, and opened the doors and hatches of the aircraft. Speaking about some additional merits of Jennifer Smith, she received the highest mark on the psychology course, which says that she can easily find a common ground with passengers and avoid any conflicts on board.

I also cannot help but mention that Miss Smith is a highly erudite person. She attended a lot of extracurricular courses outside the college and studied large volumes of literature, including specific books on the history of aviation. Also, her indisputable advantage is the fluency in several foreign languages, including French, German, and Spanish.

For me, all the above-mentioned achievements and advantages of Miss Smith are the reason for recommending her for the position of a flight attendant in your company. I do not have the slightest doubt that she will become an indispensable employee for you and a joyous experience for your passengers. Therefore, I am happy to recommend Jennifer Smith for an internship and believe that she will make the most of the opportunity she has to show her professional and personal qualities as a flight attendant in your company.

Sincerely,

Roger Patton

Acknowledgment Letter Writing Guide

Definition and Aim of an Acknowledgment Letter

An acknowledgment letter, sometimes also called a letter of receipt, is a type of formal writing used predominantly in business correspondence. There are two common types of these letters:

1. "Thank you" letter. This type of acknowledgment letter you write to your clients, partners or colleagues in order to thank them for their efforts, money, time, loyalty, and anything else they might have invested in you or your business. Such letters might also be written outside the business setting, in order to thank someone for their long-term contribution, actions, or a significant gift, but it is a less common occurrence.

2. Letter of receipt. This is a letter you send in order to let someone know you have received something they have sent you, whether it is a resume, proposition, complaint, hard copies of the documents, or a dispatch. In this case, in addition to the letter itself, you might want to send a copy of the receipt, check, or any other document confirming the delivery, or list the

items received. In this case, you send a letter as proof you have received and paid attention to what was sent to you.

In the business setting, the acknowledgment letters of both types are a vital part of establishing and maintaining efficient and friendly communication with your partners and clients.

The necessity of letters of the first type might not be apparent. Some might believe composing a text simply to say "thank you" is a waste of time for both writer and recipient. However, in business, as well as in the personal relationship, maintaining long-term relationships requires a personal touch, which you would be able to add through such letters.

A notification letter, on the other hand, is often a matter of basic courtesy: when a customer or a partner has ordered something, made a payment, or otherwise employed your service, you do not want to leave them wondering whether you will pay attention to their issue or not. This kind of letter would be more standardized and less personal, which does not mean, nevertheless, that you may forego sending them.

Taking into account that the letters of acknowledgment are usually brief, to the point, and follow a typical structure, it is a good idea to create a few templates for different occasions. In this case, composing them in the future would require making minor adjustments instead of struggling with writing from scratch every time.

Steps on How to Write an Acknowledgment Letter

Writing the acknowledgment letters might not require any creativity. However, there are some things you need to keep in mind to make your writing efficient. Here are the steps you should follow:

1. Collect all the information you might require. If you are writing a "thank you" type letter, make sure you get right names, dates, and occasions. If you write a receipt letter, verify that you do, in fact, have everything you should have received. In case you need to attach the copies of the receipts or checks, have them ready at hand.

2. It is preferable to address your recipients by their names, so if you do not know them, try to find out. Looking up the return address or the company's website should be sufficient.

3. Create an outline and a rough draft, while keeping in mind (or somewhere you can easily look it up) all the aforementioned data and documents.

4. Start with introducing yourself and state clearly why you are writing.

5. Briefly address the letter, resume, dispatch, or occurrence regarding which you are writing. Do not repeat the entire history of your previous communications, as your recipient should be well aware of it.

6. Provide all relevant information and details you want to discuss. If you are acknowledging the receipt of any documents or items, name all of them. Mentioning the date of the previous communication may also be helpful.

7. Thank the recipient for their time, efforts, interest, or anything else they have invested in you or your business during your previous communications.

8. Finish with a complimentary closing, as you would do in any other formal letter.

9. Reread and get rid of all unnecessary details, if there are any.

10. Proofread the text and make sure it contains a letterhead, your signature, and all other formal information. Also, make sure the formatting is correct.

The Structure of an Acknowledgment Letter

These letters are usually very brief and follow a typical structure which you should keep in mind.

What to Include in Your Letter

Greetings. At the very beginning of the letter, address the person you are writing to. The greetings are commonly aligned left.

In this type of letter, you would generally know exactly who the recipient is, so the greeting would look like this:

Dear Mr./Mrs. Name of the Recipient

If, however, you are not sure, you might want to address your recipient by their position, for example, *"Dear hiring manager,"* *"Dear support,"* *"Dear service,"* or, if you are responding to an order or payment, *"Dear customer."*

Introduction and the body of the letter. Considering the minimal length of the letter, it is not always possible to tell apart the introduction from the body of the letter.

However, typically, **in the first introductory part** of the letter, you should acknowledge your recipient and state the purpose of your writing, mentioning your previous communication.

In the next part, you subsequently list the items received, if there are any, and indicate which actions would be taken regarding them. For example, if you acknowledge the receipt of the resume, you may write that you or the other responsible person will examine it closely; if you are responding to an order placed, you would write that the goods will be shipped as soon as possible and so on.

Closing. In the business setting, the closing would look approximately like this:

Best regards/Respectfully,

Your Name,

Your position in the company and company name.

If your company has a standardized signature, which would be the case more often than not, by all means, use it.

Useful Expressions for Writing an Acknowledgment Letter

Acknowledgment letters belong to the type of formal writing which generally allows you to fall on clichés and set expressions. If it is a thank you letter rather than a letter of receipt, however, do not forget to include at least some personal touches. Otherwise, you will have missed the whole purpose of the letter.

Introduction and the body of the letter

- We/I would like to acknowledge the receipt of _____.

- With this letter, we hereby acknowledge receipt of your resume/documents/dispatch.

- I hereby acknowledge the receipt of the following documents _____.

- I am acknowledging receipt of your letter dated _____.

- It will be brought to his attention immediately upon (the name of the person responsible for the issue)'s return.

- We are presently examining the issue and you would receive an answer within _____ business days.

- If there are any further issues regarding _____ we will contact you within/by _____.

Closing

- If I may be of any assistance, please do not hesitate to contact me via _____.

- Thank you for your continued trust in our company.

- We look forward to doing business with you in the future.

Dos and Don'ts of Acknowledgement Letter Writing

While writing a letter of acknowledgment, you would want to keep in mind some useful tips and avoid common mistakes. Here is a list containing some of them.

Dos

- Keep your letter brief and to the point.

- Feel free to use the set expressions of the business language suitable for the occasion. However, if it is a thank you letter, it is not a good idea to make your letter consist exclusively of clichés.

- If it is a thank you letter, add a personal touch and try to be as sincere as possible.

- As with any other business letters, politeness is your best friend!

- Try if possible to address your letter to a specific person and not to an organization or company as a whole.

- Keep the tone of the letter positive. An acknowledgment letter is not a good place to bring up any issues or problems.

- Use, if possible, the company's letterhead and signature.

Don'ts

- Avoid unnecessary details, especially when you review the previous communication with the recipient. It is a good idea to remind them what exactly are you talking about, but keep it brief.

- Do not mention any negative facts or attempt to discuss any issues. Starting the letter with the expression of gratitude and ending with a list of problems or complaints would not endear you to your recipient.

- When you are writing about the actions you or your company would take, do not make any promises you cannot keep. The same goes for mentioning any dates or deadlines: make sure they are viable.

- Avoid excessive praise or compliments. This behavior would not make you look sincere and trustworthy.

Questions and Answers on Acknowledgment Letters

There are common questions regarding letters of acknowledgment which might arise while you are writing. A few of these potential questions have been addressed in question and answer format in the following section.

Q: Who might be the recipients of acknowledgment letters, and in which cases are they written?

A: Such letter may be addressed:

- to the customers of yours or your company, if you are processing their inquiry, order or complaint;

- to your colleague or employee, for example, if they are making a request or proposition, for the proceeding of which you are responsible;

- to your or your company's business partners;

- to your employer, if, for example, they have sent you documents or instructions regarding which you should take any action;

- to the potential employee, especially if you are rejecting them, but wish to acknowledge their merits or leave open the perspective of cooperation in the future.

Q: Are acknowledgment letters used outside of a business setting?

A: Yes. For example, as an individual, instead of a company representative, you might want to write to your or your children's teacher, doctor, lawyer, or, for that matter, any person who has provided you their service, for which you might feel grateful.

Works Cited

"Acknowledgement Letter, Sample Acknowledgement Letter Format." *Letters.org*, 2017,

http://www.letters.org/category/acknowledgement-letter. Accessed 15 July 2017.

Beare, Kenneth. "Business Letter Writing: Letters of Acknowledgment." *Thought Co*, 2017,

https://www.thoughtco.com/business-letter-writing-letters-of-acknowledgment-1210167.

Accessed 17 July 2017.

Heathfield, Susan M. "The Right Way to Acknowledge a Resume and Cover Letter." *The Balance*,

2016, https://www.thebalance.com/application-acknowledgement-letter-sample-1918882.

Accessed 20 July 2017.

"How to Write an Acknowledgment Letter." *Answershark.com*, 2017,

https://answershark.com/writing/business-letters/how-to-write-acknowledgment-letter.html.

Accessed 13 July 2017.

Acknowledgment Letter to Your College Professor

Return Address

John Norrington
15 Pacific St, #104
Seattle, WA 98105
United States of America

Recipient's Address

James Smith
The University of Birmingham
Edgbaston
Birmingham, B15 2TT
United Kingdom

Dear Mr. Smith,

I am writing to inform you concerning the university in Seattle which we had discussed previously in the course of my examination. I mentioned that the university offers international student scholarships available on the basis of academic excellence. Of course, scholarships at the university are awarded in a highly competitive environment, while the most successful students can expect even a full scholarship. To my delight, I was able to get it. So now I can study in the coveted university abroad and at the same time remain financially independent of my family. I am acknowledging your significant contribution in that success. Indeed, the preparation process was challenging, but I have realized the advantages of your critical thinking approach to learning. It would have been challenging to pass entrance tests successfully without the skill of reflection and knowledge in the scope of international affairs and politics.

Furthermore, it is difficult to count all of the advantages which were opened before me due to this scholarship. The university is on the list of the best and oldest educational institutions in the country, and some of its programs separately deserve a high-quality assessment. Thus, the

30

university's programs of my particular interest in the field of jurisprudence are included in the national top, and the bachelor's and master's programs in international relations rank highly even in world rankings. Separately, it is worth mentioning the role of media and information technology in the university. Students here learn from real professionals, including CNN and BBC media journalists and well-known political analysts.

Another characteristic of the university, which is important for all students, is the availability of different opportunities for passing working practices and the responsiveness of teachers. After learning from you, I understand how important it is to have a qualitative dialogue between the student and the teacher. In addition, unlike many universities, the scholarship at the university also covers the cost of accommodation. Concerning accommodation, it is provided not only to first-year students. On the contrary, the university makes it possible for students to stay in residence during the entire period of study in the bachelor's program.

Furthermore, the undoubted advantage of the University is its location near a variety of cultural and historical sites. This allows students to actively develop and gain new knowledge even outside the university walls. By the way, all the campuses of the University take security very seriously. There operates its police station, whose employees are supporting the order. Thus, I can ensure you that this scholarship has opened the way for me not only to study but also to have excellent conditions for living and scientific progress.

Finally, there are also a lot of scientific centers here, and I think that I will continue to develop the project that we started together regarding the role of the media in Arab Spring and other significant civil movements and uprisings. Of course, I will need your support as an experienced specialist, so I hope that we will continue correspondence. Moreover, the university was pleasantly surprised by the recommendation letter that you provided, since your publications are widely known even here.

All in all, please accept my kindest gratitude regarding your support and help in this challenging process. At last, please remember that if I can assist you in any way, do not hesitate to call or contact me.

Sincerely,

John Norrington

Acknowledgment Letter for a Kickstarter Project

Dear Mr. Padington,

It was a great surprise to reveal your strong support of our Kickstarter project of innovative heated clothing. I am acknowledging your significant contribution to the development of the project since it is now possible to consider some ideas which were previously ignored due to expectations of a reduced budget.

Thus, I would like to tell you more details about our activities. Meanwhile, the products focused on heating limbs remain a priority. These products include socks, insoles, and gloves. I find it necessary to send you some prototypes of future models to persuade you regarding the validity of your donation. Furthermore, it is paramount to recall some primary advantages. The heating elements consist of soft and flexible carbon heating plates, which provide stable and safe heating. Nevertheless, our team expects that the collection of sponsorship funds will continue to rise, and there are ready-made concepts and sketches, as well as the design of a line of outerwear. I will send them with prototypes as well to you.

Furthermore, in addition to the advantages, there is the strength of the heating elements since punching or folding will not ruin them. Another plus is the ease of use due to the utilization of innovative compact lithium-ion batteries with a high power charge that lasts for a week. Finally, all elements are waterproof. The process itself is based on the technology of infrared radiation. In addition to the heating process, this radiation is extremely useful for a person as the circulation of blood increases, as well as the speed of recovery processes. Since this idea affects health, I would like to know your opinion on one component that could improve the technological part of the project; the only issue is the fact that it requires additional costs.

The team actively considers the function of health monitoring. Thanks to the built-in modules, clothes would measure the primary indicators including heart rate, pressure, temperature, and others. Also, it is possible to add wireless data transfer, and the personal doctor will always be aware of the basic health indicators. I will be grateful for the advice on this idea.

All in all, please, accept my kindest gratitude regarding your donation and help in our attempt to develop smart technologies. Please do not hesitate to call or contact me in the case of any questions.

Best regards,

Jack Parkson

Adjustment Letter Writing Guide

Definition and Aim of an Adjustment Letter

An adjustment letter, in the business setting, is a letter you write as a representative of your company to address a complaint or claim of the customer. This letter is also commonly referred to as a complaint response letter, customer complaint reply, or a claim adjustment letter. This type of writing covers the response to the wide range of the possible complaints and causes for dissatisfaction: poor service, faulty or damaged goods, shipments being lost or delivered late, and so on.

In the context of the customer-vendor relation, an adjustment letter is, first of all, a way to maintain the good relationships with the dissatisfied customer. Additionally, it is also a legal document, which serves as a testimony to the details of the previous correspondence, as well as to the solution or dissolution of the issue at hand.

The principal aim of the adjustment letter is to notify the recipient that their complaint or claim was received and was (or will be) processed. In the case the customer's claim is found to be valid, and you or your company have done or are planning to do something about it, it is a good idea to tell your respondent about it. However, if you are not sure or if the claim is proven to be invalid, you should stick to apologizing and informing the customer that their claim is received. It is obvious that you should not make any promises you would not be able to carry out, regardless of how strong your wish to appease the customer might be. So, in your letter, you should acknowledge the problem, apologize, and offer some type of reconciliation in order to restore the customer's good will.

Adjustment letters should be treated as a significant part of your company's marketing and public relations. Your writing might decide whether your company is to be trusted and whether the customer would consider employing your service again. In certain circumstances, with a well-written adjustment letter, you might be able not only to rectify the customer's impression of your company but even boost their confidence in it and promote the future cooperation.

Steps on How to Write an Adjustment Letter

Adjustment letters are a formal type of writing, and follow a rather rigid structure which lacks creativity. It requires, nevertheless, a bit of a personal touch, as you want to maintain good relations with the customer, especially if their complaint is valid. There are some important steps you should consider while writing an adjustment letter.

1. Before starting to write, make sure you have ready at hand both the customer's original letter and any information regarding the decisions on the issues you would need to tell your respondent. In case you need to attach any documents, copies of checks or notifications, you should also have them prepared.

2. You might want to create a bullet point list of the issues your letter would cover. It is especially important if you need to ask the customer to entertain any further actions, for example, to send back the damaged goods, receive the inspection, or fill some forms.

3. Start your letter with a positive statement. Depending on the situation, you might say you are pleased to hear from the customer, express sympathy regarding the reasons for their complaint, or both.

4. Refer the date of the original complaint or claim and explain you are writing as a response to it.

5. Recap and discuss the issue which has caused the complaint. You would not want to go into too many details, as the customer will most likely remember what their problem was. Nevertheless, you should demonstrate that you have paid attention and understood the issue and are not brushing it off.

6. Provide a factual explanation. If the complaint is valid and there are any circumstances which might exonerate or justify your company's mistake, explain them. If, however, the claim is invalid, respectfully explain why it is so.

7. Give the decision regarding the claim. If it is valid, you should explicitly recognize this fact and then express the apologies as sincerely as possible. Then you should discuss the measures which would be employed to rectify the mistake, compensation, and any other steps your company would take. Be specific here.

8. If the claim is invalid, try to explain this as delicately as you can and, if it is possible, offer some substitute compensation which might satisfy the customer.

9. Finish your writing on a positive note. You might express the hope that the customer would continue employing your company's service.

10. Proofread the letter, get rid of any unnecessary details, and make sure your grammar and punctuation are flawless and your tone of address is polite and friendly.

The Structure of an Adjustment Letter

The letters of adjustment serve a very particular purpose, and as you would likely need to write many of them, you should keep in mind their typical structure.

What to Include in Your Letter

Greetings. First of all, you address your recipient, stating their name and the title. In this type of letter, you would generally know who are you writing to, as the letters of complaint would be signed. In this case, your mode of greeting would be:

Dear Mr./Mrs. Last Name

If you cannot determine the gender of the recipient based on their name, you would address them as "Dear First Name Last Name."

If it happens so that you do not know the name of the recipient, your chosen mode of address would be "Dear customer."

Introduction. In the introduction, you should refer to the initial complaint and state that you are writing in response to it. You may also express sympathy, apologize for the inconvenience or express gratitude for getting in touch with your company and helping to attract the attention to the issue.

The body of the letter. In the body of the letter, which is typically between one and three paragraphs long, you should briefly discuss the problem in order to show the customer you have comprehended their complaint and paid attention to it. Then you should provide, if possible, an explanation of the causes of the issue. In the end, you will inform the customer of the decision regarding their case and discuss any actions which were taken or will be taken to address the issue.

Closing. In the closing paragraph, you may once again apologize and express the hope the customer would continue doing business with you.

To sign your letter, you would generally use the mode of signature established by your company. If there is none, you would conclude with "Best regards" or "Respectfully," following by your name, your position, and your company's name.

Useful Expressions for Writing an Adjustment Letter

Introduction

- We thank you for your letter dated _____.

- We have received your recent letter dated (month, date, year) concerning the _____.

- It is important to us to know of issues that arise with our customers.

- Thank you for writing and giving us an opportunity to look into this matter.

The body of the letter

- We regret this mistake.

- We apologize for any inconveniences we might have caused you.

- I would like to assure you of our interest and concern.

- The mistake has occurred because of _____.

- We are always anxious to be informed of_____.

- We apologize for the situation that has evolved.

- We realize that this is a substantial problem.

- We filed a concern with (the problem that was caused) and are waiting for their solution.

- We had no other concerns regarding (this type of problems) so this may be an individual case.

- You can expect the full reimbursement within_____.

- We are quite sure that your request for the adjustment/compensation will be granted.

- You can, of course, return the item to us and receive full compensation/debit our account for the loss caused to you.

Closing

- We are sorry you/your company suffered the consequences____.

- We would like to offer you (type of compensation) as an apology.

- Please accept our apology for the____.

- We promise that we will improve our____.

- We will do our best to avoid such problems in the future.

- I hope this unfortunate accident will not keep you from employing our company's services in the future.

- We again regret the inconvenience to you.

Dos and Don'ts of Adjustment Letter Writing

Here are some tips you would want to remember in order to make your adjustment letter writing efficient.

Dos

- Adopt the "you" attitude.

- Remain polite even if the complaint sounds extremely belligerent and accusatory.

- Try to explain the situation and provide details regarding its solution.

- Explicitly admit if the customer is right.

- If the company is guilty, accept it, try to explain the causes, but avoid shifting the blame or making empty excuses.

- Be specific and to the point.

Don'ts

- At all costs, avoid sounding flippant or dismissive. Even if the complaint is invalid, the customer should believe their issue was given the necessary consideration and taken seriously.

- Do not rush to tell "no" to the customer. Even if their claim is invalid, you should deliver it delicately and after the positive introduction.

- Do not make promises you have no opportunity, power or intention to carry out.

- Do not use professional jargon or any ambiguous or obscure language.

- Avoid overusing passive voice.

- Do not restate the initial issue in the closing paragraph. You should finish on a positive note.

Questions and Answers on Adjustment Letters

There are common questions regarding the adjustment letters, the answers to some of which you can find here.

Q: How do I soften the blow if the complaint is invalid?

A: If it is possible in the particular case and within the limits of your company's policy, you might offer some substitute or partial compensation. Otherwise, just do your best to be diplomatic, tactful, and provide the reasons for rejecting the customer's claim, so they at least would be sure you have paid attention to it and examined the case.

Q: What is "you attitude" and why is it helpful?

A: In your writing, try to shift the focus on the customer instead of yourself and your company. If it is possible, write, for example, "you would receive an item" instead of "I have sent an item." This is a useful tool in making the customer feel appreciated and cared about.

Q: Should I use the "I" or "we" pronoun in my letter?

A: There is ambiguous advice on this matter. Many fall back on the default "we," while others consider that "I" would sound more friendly and intimate. So, strictly speaking, it's up to you. You might want to take into consideration, however, the specifics of your position in the company. If you are the customer service manager and it is your responsibility to deal with the complaints and ensure the resolution of the matter, you might use "I." If you are speaking on behalf of the whole company, however, and want to stress this point, "we" would be more appropriate.

Works Cited

Gerald J. Alred, Charles T. Brusaw, and Walter E. Oliu. *The Business Writer's Handbook*, 10th ed.

    Macmillan, 2011. Accessed 1 July 2017.

"How to Write an Adjustment Letter." *Answershark.com,* 2017,

    https://answershark.com/writing/business-letters/how-to-write-adjustment-letter.html.

    Accessed 3 July 2017.

Nordquist, Richard. "Characteristics of an Effective Adjustment Letter." *ThoughtCo*, 2017,

    https://www.thoughtco.com/what-is-adjustment-letter-1688973. Accessed 5 July 2017.

Nordquist, Richard. "Why Good Business Writing Should Be All About You (Not Me)."

    ThoughtCo, 2017, https://www.thoughtco.com/adopting-the-you-attitude-professional-

    writing-1691781. Accessed 3 July 2017.

Walton, Sam M. "Adjustment Letter." *University of Arkansas. College of Business,*

    https://walton.uark.edu/business-communication-lab/Resources/downloads/business-

    forms/Adjustment_Letter.pdf. Accessed 1 July 2017.

Writing@CSU. "Adjustment Letters." *Colorado State University. The Writing Studio,* 2017,

    https://writing.colostate.edu/guides/page.cfm?pageid=1462&guideid=71. Accessed 1 July

    2017.

Adjustment Letter for a Young Adult – Customer Credit Refusal

Return Address

John Maria Juanita Alba Lopez
Client Service Department
Philips Bank for Investments and Savings
10660 Hammerly Blvd
Houston, TX 77043

Recipient's Address

Laura Palmer
1205 Broadway St, #205
Vancouver, WA 98666

Dear Laura Palmer,

We have received your request for a new loan dated June 5, 2017. We are grateful for the credit application that you have made. Nonetheless, we are obligated to refuse your loan request.

After reviewing your application carefully, we have established that it does not meet the criteria necessary for the credit approval. Even though you have a sufficient work record, educational background, and income level, we have to reject your request because of several delayed credit card payments in your credit history.

As you probably understand, delinquent payments can jeopardize your credit history. We cannot approve your new loan requests as long as you have not overtaken your arrears. Now, you have three delinquent payments that amount to $500 in total. With such amount of money still unpaid, we cannot grant you the new credit.

With this letter, we would also like to kindly remind you to pay off your delayed credit card payments. You have already received three notices encouraging you to settle your arrears; nonetheless, we have obtained no payments to pay off the debt. Please take into consideration that postponing settling your arrears affects your credit record negatively. Thus, we encourage you to pay attention to your delinquent payments and pay off your debt as soon as possible.

M. N. K. Philips Bank for Investments and Savings' policy is friendly towards the young people. We also understand that, as a young adult, you were particularly vulnerable to financial difficulties. Our company aims to meet the requirements of its clients and to assist them in managing financial hardship. Thereby, if some pressing circumstances do not allow you to pay off your debt, please, inform us so that we can look for other payment options. For example, if you are sick, you can send us a notice from your doctor that confirms your diagnosis. If the costs of the treatment are high, we can delay the payment. Furthermore, we also can postpone the payment in case of unemployment. Therefore, if you were recently fired and had no funds to pay the debts, we can delay the payment for a few months.

What is more, we would like to inform you about our Social Responsibility Program. M. N. K. Philips Bank for Investments and Savings understands the necessity of supporting vulnerable categories of the population. We believe that, except for earning a profit, big businesses should contribute to the well-being of American society. We respect diversity and understand that particular societal groups have been oppressed in the past. Consequently, we can write off 20% of the debt, if you belong to one of the following groups:

- women

- ethnical minorities

- sexual minorities

- people with disabilities

- working class people

If you have any further questions or information that could confirm your belonging to one of these groups, feel free to contact us.

After you pay this sum off, you can reapply for the credit. It is likely that we will approve your request after you successfully overtake your arrears.

Sincerely,

Maria Juanita Alba Lopez
Credit Collector,
Client Service Department
M. N. K. Philips Bank for Investments and Savings

Adjustment Letter – The Service of Tiger Restaurant

Return Address

Mr. Leonard Hofstadter
Customer Service Manager
Head Office of Tiger Restaurant
620 Atlantic Ave
Brooklyn, NY 11217

Recipient's Address

Mr. Sheldon Cooper
450 Flatbush Ave, #110
Brooklyn, NY 11225

Dear Mr. Cooper,

We have received your recent letter dated June 12, 2017, concerning the service of Tiger Restaurant on June 11, 2017. Our restaurant thanks you for your letter, gives us a chance to look through this matter. It is of crucial importance for us to know all of the issues which the customers of Tiger Restaurant have with our service. We are always working to ensure full customer satisfaction. We have examined all the circumstances of the issue that took place on June 11, 2017. We appreciate your claim and will try to find proper solution to the problem that has arisen.

Mr. Wolowitz, who was your waiter that day and whose work is the basis of your complaint, has been an employee of Tiger Restaurant for five years. He is one of the best among our waiters and has an excellent reputation among our customers. For his entire career at Tiger Restaurant, there have been no unfavorable incidents connected with his behavior and work.

There are several factors have preceded the behavior of Mr. Wolowitz, which at first glance, could be mistakenly deemed as "unprofessional." It was an extremely busy day, where all the tables were reserved and occupied. Our waiter served several tables, which is one of the causes of why he mistook the orders and brought you the wrong dishes. We are very sorry for the spoiled dress of your wife after Mr. Wolowitz inadvertently spilled a plate of soup on her.

After examining the video record, we have come to understand that it was an unpleasant coincidence. Another visitor in a hurry pushed our waiter, and Mr. Wolowitz, unable to retain balance, spilled soup on the dress. We perfectly understand that there is no fault to be leveled against you, which is why our restaurant will compensate for the full cost of your wife's dress. As we came to understand further, the waiter could not apologize in that moment because he suddenly felt sick. Mr. Wolowitz is diabetic, and suffered from hypoglycemia at that particular moment. We assure you that, previously, this fact did not prevent our employee from working effectively. We will talk to him and test him for professional suitability for further cooperation. We would like to assure you that we are interested in all the issues that take place in our restaurant. We are always anxious to prevent all situations that can spoil our relations with customers.

We appreciate you as our customer, and we do not want to lose you. We will try to do everything to make amends for this unfortunate accident. In addition to covering the costs of replacing the dress, we would like to offer you three free visits to our restaurant for you and your family. In addition, you will be able to order any beverages from our bar. Your presence in our restaurant is significant for us. We hope that you will be sympathetic to the situation that has developed. We will be glad to see you and your family in Tiger Restaurant.

Sincerely,

Mr. Leonard Hofstadter
Customer Service Manager

Application Letter Writing Guide

Definition and Aim of an Application Letter

A letter of application is often an attachment to a resume for a job, but also is used when enrolling in a university, college or short-term courses.

The aim of the letter is to introduce yourself to a potential employee or committee, providing and highlighting your personal qualities and qualifications. It is a kind of marketing tool that helps the employer directly see your skills and experience. Also, this letter demonstrates that you have spent some amount of time to customize information according to their needs. A resume that is accompanied with an application letter will increase your chances to be chosen for a job interview, or with obtaining the desired position or place in the selected university.

In fact, not all employees have time for reading every application letter. But how will you know that you will be on the list? Attach this letter in any case. To ease your work, create a standardized application letter that can be simply transformed into a specific one when you address a new company.

Steps on How to Write an Application Letter

How to write an application letter and stand out among the crowd of applicants? How to convince the committee that your candidacy is the best choice? Basically, every employer and university committee has some basic information they want to see. That's why it is important to follow a certain strategy while writing your application letter.

1. Get prepared. Gather all information about yourself: your education and your personal and professional qualities. Think about what job you want and why you need it. Think about what you can present to stand out. Contact those people that will be your referee and ask them to confirm their contact information.

2. Examine the employer. Read the job description and find out what qualities and experience you should have in order to be chosen. Also check the deadline for applying for vacancy. If you submit your candidature early, you will have more chances to be noticed.

3. Write the subject or a heading with information. Write the name of vacancy you are applying for in the subject field of your email, so the employer will clearly detect your mail from others. For example:

Subject: James Drake, Product Manager Position.

 If you are sending a traditional letter, list your address, date and name in the left margin.

4. Address the letter. If possible, address your letter to the specific person that is in charge of hiring and interviewing. This will increase your chances to be seriously reviewed by the company.

5. Write the body paragraph. It may be divided into three paragraphs. First paragraph will grab the reader's attention and give the main reason why you are applying for this certain university or job. Second paragraph will be about your personal qualities and your accomplishments. Third paragraph is about what bonuses university or company will receive with choosing your candidacy. At the end you should ask for a meeting or call. Here are some questions that you can answer.

For university admission:

- Where did you find out about the university and the program? What attracts you to study here?

- What are your strong personal and academic qualities?

- What is your experience, and how will it help you to study in the chosen course?

- What goals do you plan to achieve by studying here?

- Why exactly are you suitable for this university and for this program?

For employment:

- Where did you learn about this company and the vacancy?

- Why does this company and the vacancy fit you? What is attracting you?

- What are your strong personal and professional qualities?

- What is your experience, and how will it help you successfully work in this place?

- What goals do you plan to achieve by working here?

- Why do you need to take this position?

6. Show your arguments. Carefully choose points to persuade the company that you are the most suitable candidate. In this paragraph you should show the reader that you have the required skills. Explain how the company will benefit from hiring you and why they should start a relationship with you. At the end of the letter, indicate which accompanying documents you have attached to the letter.

7. Write the signature. After the text of your letter it is necessary to say goodbye. Begin by leaving one blank line, as the signature section should be separated from the text of the letter. Write on a separate line an appeal: "Regards," "Best regards," or "Sincerely yours" if you want. And on the second separate line – your full name.

8. Write contact details. If you are sending an email, mention your contact details at the end of the letter: name, address, email address and telephone number so the recruiter will easily get in touch with you.

9. Check over your letter. Proofread your application letter with focused attention. Put the letter aside for a few days and reread it. Most likely, you will find new grammar errors or sentences that need improvements. Also you can give your application letter to friends and ask for their suggestions.

10. Consider before sending. Reread your resume and application letter for the last time. Check the requirements of the job posting, and if it requires both a resume and application letter as an attachment, make sure that you used Adobe PDF files or Microsoft Word. Don't forget to title the file with your name and vacancy title, i.e. jamesdrakeresume.doc, jamesdrakecover.doc.

The Structure of an Application Letter

What to Include in Your Letter

Here is a list of moments you should include in your application letter. Make sure that you cover them in the proper order. Following this structure, you will make your letter a lot easier to read and to understand your story. Feel free to add anything you think will increase your chances, but remember that you have a limit – your application letter should be not more than one page.

Subject (if you plan to send an email) or contact information at the top:

Name

Address

City, State, zip code

Phone number

Email address

Date

Greeting. Here you have two options that depend on situation:

1) If you know the name of person that will be reading your letter, write:

Dear Mr./Mrs. Last Name

Dear Professor Smith

2) In case if you don't know the gender, you can write full name without the title:

Dear Janie Brown

3) If you don't know the name and it's impossible to find out, write general salutation:

Dear Sir or Madam

Dear hiring manager

Body of application letter

The body of your letter lets the committee know what scientific field you are interested in and why the university should select you among other students.

- First paragraph

The first paragraph lets the committee understand why you have chosen the particular university. Make your goal clear and give a short preview of your letter. Why do you think the university program is suitable and interesting for you?

- Middle paragraph

Focus on your previous education and skills. Tell a short story about your experience and background in the field. Mention those qualifications that will be most suitable to the program. Refer to your CV for more details if needed.

- Last paragraph

Restate your interest and ask for a personal interview if suitable. Give thanks for the chance to show yourself in this letter.

Complimentary close

Sincerely,

Signature (for a mailed letter)

Contact information (for email)

Useful Expressions for Writing an Application Letter

Phrases to Use		
The Aim of Letter	**Qualifications**	**Ending**
I am writing to apply for admission to the course in..	I hold a certificate/degree in...	I would be glad to attend an interview at any time convenient to you.
I would like to be considered for a place of...	I have taken/passed examination...	I hope that you will consider me for entry/admission to...
I am writing with regard to...	I have completed the following courses / degree course...	I hope that you will consider my application...
I am writing to apply for... which I saw advertised in...	I enclose / have enclosed a copy of my degree/diploma...	I hope you take a favorable decision regarding my application for...

Dos and Don'ts of an Application Letter Writing

When you have only 20 seconds to catch the attention of a committee member or employer that is reading your application letter, even a little mistake may spoil the first impression. As soon as you will finish writing the letter, please consider the following points.

Dos

- Adhere to a formal style and write short and to the point. Use simple, clean fonts, such as Arial or Times New Roman with font size 10-12 pt and single-space the text. Ideally, the letter should be very short — busy people do not read long letters. But it should be as informative and emotional as possible.

- The summary should be in chronological record, telling about your educational and business experience.

- Explain the reasons of unemployed periods in your resume. It is also advised to explain the reasons for the frequent change of work. In general, try to predict the questions that the hiring manager may have about your resume and answer them in advance. This will be the right strategy.

- Keep an optimistic and emotional tone in the letter. It attracts attention.

Don'ts

- Don't write a letter longer than one page. Your reader will feel bored and your letter won't be considered.

- Don't repeat the information in the application letter and the resume. The application letter should show your motivation, leadership qualities, ambitions, plans, and personal qualities.

- Don't criticize your current place of work, previous work, boss or co-workers.

- Don't use unprofessional jargon. Carefully check the grammar and style of the letter – there is nothing worse than an illiterate and carelessly written application letter.

- Don't state salary requirements in your application form if the employer doesn't require it.

Questions and Answers on Application Letters

Every application letter is unique and writing one is a quite a challenging process even for an excellent student. We have answers for the most frequently asked questions to make the process of writing easier.

Q: What length should an application letter be?

A: Most often, two mistakes occur:

Too long text may seem boring, and it will fly into the recycle bin. For a long listing of your merits and experience, use a summary. The same can be said about long paragraphs – avoid them.

Too short text — you will create the impression of a person who is not interested in this vacancy. Show your sincere enthusiasm, the desire to work precisely on this position! The length of an application letter should be read in about 30 seconds. This is about 3 to 5 paragraphs, with a maximum of 3-6 lines each.

Q: How should I apply to the recipient?

A: Preferably, you should find out the name of the person you will be writing to. In this case, you will write like this: "Dear Mr. Smith." If you don't know the name, avoid writing "All concerned" or "Sir or Madam" as it looks too common. Try to find out the name of the responsible person by phone. If this quest will be impracticable, write at the top left corner "Application Letter" without addressing the recipient.

Q: How should I put the address on the letter?

A: Usually it is placed in the right margin and includes the following information:

- Your name

- Mailing address

- Email

- Contact phone number

Q: Should I send an email or a letter by mail?

A: You have the possibility of trying both options, but we advise you to send an email for several reasons:

- Internet is the most popular way of communication

- You can do it from home

- It will be delivered in a second

The only disadvantage is that your mail may be delivered as junk mail, but this possibility is very low.

Q: Should I attach the letter or put it in the body of my email?

A: We recommend you to put the text of your application letter in the body of the email when sending your resume as an attachment. When your potential employer will open the email, your letter will give the first impression. They will encounter a professional text that gives them an additional reason to open and read your resume.

Q: Do I need to write my "objective" in the application letter?

A: It is not necessary — you can just state the position you are applying for.

Every person that writes an application letter should take in mind that the text he or she creates should interest the reader from the very beginning. Search for your unique qualities, present it in written form, leave it aside and then proofread. Take enough time, as you need a lot of concentration. A good application letter will be successful if you are really interested in the desired university program or job position. Believe in yourself even if you fail for the first time. Just keep on trying and improving until you achieve success!

Works Cited

Breen, Peter. *The Book of Letters: How to Write a Letter for Every Occasion.* Crows Nest,

N.S.W.: Allen & Unwin, 2002. Accessed 11 July 2017.

Kaplan, Robbie Miller. *How to Say It in Your Job Search: Choice Words, Phrases, Sentences,*

and Paragraphs for Resumes, Cover Letters, and Interviews. Paramus, NJ: Prentice Hall

Press, 2002. Accessed 12 July 2017.

Maggio, Rosalie. *How to Say It: Choice Words, Phrases, Sentences, and Paragraphs for Every*

Situation. Englewood Cliffs, NJ: Prentice Hall, 1990. Accessed 11 July 2017.

Strunk, William, and Stanford, Pritchard. *The Elements of Style.* Middlebury, VT: Springside,

2012. Accessed 12 July 2017.

Roman, Kenneth, and Joel Raphaelson. *Writing That Works: How to Communicate Effectively in*

Business: Email, Letters, Memos, Presentations, Plans, Reports, Proposals, Resumes,

Speeches. New York: HarperCollins, 2000. Accessed 12 July 2017.

Application Letter to a Medical College

Return Address

Elisabet Taylor
10 Queen's Street
London
SW1W 9LX

Recipient's Address

John Howe
London School of Hygiene & Tropical Medicine
15 Keppel Street
London
WC1E 7HT

Dear Mr. Howe,

This letter is with reference to the medical program offered by your college. I would like to enter my dream college. Therefore, I am writing to you with a full heart of hope.

The medical program you are offering will be a nice opportunity to gain the proper level of knowledge to become a qualified professional in the medical sphere. I have some experience in this field and I hope to do much more with your help. I have participated in a school contest and achieved the first place. The task was to create a cell that would be inserted into the body in the place affected by cancerous cells.

The cell I created is a cancer vaccine and has already helped people in need of it. In fact, I hope your college will help me in creating and designing such vaccines that can be a real cure for our world. These medicines can become one of the least expensive and at the same time necessary treatments in the world. This is my goal to achieve and my dream to follow. To help people who suffer from incurable diseases and to find the particular treatment to each of them is my desire and wish. Therefore, I am absolutely sure that entering your medical college is the best option I can truly imagine. Moreover, I believe that all of these key points can help in achieving this dream.

Furthermore, I would like to highlight that finding the right college to gain the proper knowledge is a complicated task that demands a lot of work and time. However, I consider that your policy is closely connected with my strengths and desires. For example, I am fond of your policy of giving the students practical experience. As a matter of fact, I believe that practical experience in the medical sphere is the most important factor in choosing the college to enter. And thus, I think that this is the strong and firm advantage and benefit of your college's policy. Moreover, I believe that this benefit is helpful in my views on the educational process. This means that we will become a great team!

In addition, I would like to point out that the more I know the inner policy of your college, the more I am persuaded that we can help each other become better people in this world. For example, I have to say I am a creative person and I am fond of designing biological and medical models. Your college can provide me with the theoretical basis, while I can continue to create the models of the medical world and we will become the most influential combination of today's world.

Finally, I hope to become a part of your medical college community and find my own place in this exciting and amusing world of medical progress. Moreover, I suppose that the knowledge of your university will give me the opportunity to find the world of my dreams. Therefore, it could become a great contribution to the world of genetics, biology, and medicine.

Sincerely,

Elisabet

Application Letter – Rising Talent Scholarship

Return Address

Sarah Hanks
1031 Hillside Drive, #456
Bloomington, IN 47401

Recipient's Address

Theresa May
Head of Scholarship Committee
Indiana University Jacobs School of Music
205 S Jordan Ave
Bloomington, IN 47405

Dear Mrs. May,

I was inspired to learn about the Rising Talent Scholarship that was announced at the Indiana University Jacobs School of Music. It corresponds to my dream and goal to begin the career of a solo singer and to pursue a degree in a successful institution with broad abilities. I have always dreamed of studying at this university because my parents loved music and I have grown up nearby in the atmosphere of art and songs. Simultaneously, I have practiced singing since I was a kid. Today, this scholarship may allow me to realize both my dreams and learning opportunities.

I think that music and singing have always been my passion. Moreover, my aunt was a quite well-known artist in our town before her tragic passing, and she loved to sing with me and prompt my future as a star. So I was living in this dream, and not only sang for relaxation or hobby, but started to master the voice, its tones, opportunities, and power. By completing my degree, I will not only make a positive contribution to my career but find many highly-acclaimed teachers, people willing to help me to develop those aspects of my voice which are challenging. At the same time, I will also pay tribute to my aunt as she tried her best every time she started a performance, and it became my golden rule as well. Being a singer holds a great deal of importance to me.

Regarding my success and background, I need to admit that I have graduated Bradbury High School in Charlotte, Indiana with honors and comparative success in art activities. During the years of education, I have participated in several significant contests and even won an Audience Award at the Indiana Young Talents Contest. Moreover, I have tried to cooperate with social projects conducted in the school and performed shortly at charity events, since it allowed me to implement the purpose of music. I have always believed that music is called to bring emotions, rhythm, passion, or mood, and there is no better way to communicate with the audience and express the deepest emotions than singing. Nevertheless, I also was an enthusiastic student at my high school. Thus, I was involved in student self-government and developed several significant social sciences projects in the sphere of people's preferences in music.

In general, the scholarship is ideal for me, and it will allow not only to use the broad base of your university for training, but also to live, learn, develop the voice with the best teachers of the country, and make a childhood dream come true. Altogether, it seems to me an ideal combination for an active young life. Moreover, my priority tasks are to give people emotions, feelings, and moving experiences, and in this regard, the scholarship can help me too.

Finally, I hope that you will consider my application. It really will help me apply all my strengths to improve my skills and promote the development of the university, which became my alma mater when I was only 10 years old. Looking forward to your reply.

Sincerely,

Sarah Hanks

Complaint Letter Writing Guide

Definition and Aim of a Complaint Letter

A formal letter of complaint is written if you want to alert the company about a problem and express the dissatisfaction with its products or services. Usually, it is used when all other means, such as verbal requests or phone calls, are exhausted. You may encounter the need to write a letter of complaint both as a private person and as a representative of your company. Writing such a letter is a powerful way to influence the company responsible for some violation, and therefore to protect you from violations of customer's rights, or dissatisfactory quality of goods or services.

In most cases, it is in the company's interests to address the issue in order to avoid losing its customers. Take into account that your letter of complaint is first and foremost not an outlet for your anger and frustration, but rather a piece of formal writing with which you are trying to achieve some specific goal, namely prompting the company or organization to change something. Therefore, regardless of whether you are writing on behalf of your company or yourself, you should approach writing the complaint letter with rationality and a cool head.

In most cases, consumer protection agencies, the Better Business Bureau, and similar organizations encourage customers to address the companies directly with their problems and issues, and more often than not, if the complaint is valid, companies would be more than happy to rectify their mistakes.

Steps on How to Write a Complaint Letter

To make sure your letter of complaint is efficient and to the point, consider following these steps while writing:

1. Start with collecting all necessary information. Take a photo or scan the check, make a screenshot of an online transaction, ask the bank for the information on your funds movements, take a photo of the product. Note its serial number, any invoice-numbers or customer reference numbers, manufacture and/or purchase date, and any previous communications. All of this will be necessary to provide the factual proof of your claim, and it is likely you will need to enclose a lot of information in your letter, so you may consider creating a separate folder with everything you need so you will have it at hand.

2. Visit the company's website or give them a call and, if necessary, find out to whom exactly you should address your complaint.

3. Begin the letter with briefly introducing yourself and your issue.

4. Provide detailed information on your issue. State which product or service you will be talking about, then describe what exactly is wrong with it. You may also discuss what problems this has caused you to stress the importance of resolving the issue.

5. Indicate how you want to resolve the issue and which steps, in your opinion, the company should take. If you want a refund, replacement, apology, and so on, state it explicitly.

6. Indicate how long you are going to wait for the company's response before you seek the help of a third party. Normally, the term is no less than two weeks to allow the company time for the action.

7. Try to finish the letter on a positive note, expressing the hope the issue will be resolved quickly and for mutual satisfaction.

8. Don't forget to enclose all necessary files and documents!

The Structure of a Complaint Letter

What to Include in Your Letter

It is not every day that you write complaint letters, so it is natural if you struggle with the content. Here are some tips on what to include in your letter to ensure its efficiency.

Greetings. It is advisable that you address your letter to someone with authority who can help you to resolve your issue. In these cases, there are chances that you will find the name of the person in charge on the company's website or by phone, and in this instance, you will use the good old "Dear Mr./Mrs. Last Name." However, it is common to not know whom exactly you are writing to. If this is the case, you can use the more generic "Dear Sir or Madam." The complaint letter is one of the rare instances when even "To Whom It May Concern" is acceptable, as with this letter you aim to be as formal as possible.

Introduction. In the introductory paragraph, you briefly identify yourself, for example, as a customer of the company, and clearly state the reason you are writing. Do not go into too many details just yet, but indicate that you are dissatisfied with the quality of the products or services the company provides and that you want to complain.

The body of the letter. In the main part of your letter, you discuss the issue and the possible ways to resolve it. First of all, indicate the product or the service you have the issue with. Be as specific as possible and provide a serial number, manufacturing date, and any other data which will make it easier to identify what you are talking about.

Then, describe what exactly the issue is. If you are talking about damaged or malfunctioning goods, describe the problem in detail. If you have issues with the company's service or if you have had any previous communication regarding it, provide a brief recap and a timeline of what is going on. Describe the inconveniences or the damage the issue has caused you.

At last, use a separate paragraph to discuss the possible ways of resolving the issue. Be specific and do not beat around the bush. If you want a refund or exchange, write so — do not expect the company to take the initiative.

Closing. In the closing paragraph, you express the hope that your issue will be resolved in due time and warn the company of the measures you will take otherwise. Provide your contact information to make it possible to get in touch with you after the company comes to a decision. Try to be courteous here and if there is a chance you will still do business with this company or use their service, express the hope your good relations with it will be restored.

Useful Expressions for Writing a Complaint Letter

It may not be easy for you to find the right words to describe your problem, and, as a letter of complaint hardly requires any creativity, some phrases and set expressions, the examples of which are provided here, can be most helpful.

Introduction

- I am a customer of (the name of the company) and I am concerned about the services you offer.

- I am writing to complain of the poor service I received from your company on the (date).

- I would hereby like to lodge a complaint for____.

- I am writing this letter to inform you of various malfunctions with____.

The body of the letter

- I am afraid that your company's performance was disappointing.

- I have not received my purchase, despite the promise to deliver it (within the time frame).

- The delay of the product has caused me many inconveniences.

- It is now the _____ time that I have registered a complaint with your company.

- To resolve the problem, I would appreciate receiving a refund.

- The company should contact me within (the time frame).

- My strongest belief is that the company will see the problem _____.

- I believe your company will get back to me with the decision (within the time frame).

- The refundable money includes_____.

- It is quite unfortunate that your service was inadequate, because _____.

- I would appreciate if I get another (name of the product) as a replacement, otherwise, I will ask for a refund.

Closing

- I am looking forward to your reply and a resolution to my problem.

- Please contact me at _____.

- Please, take appropriate measures to avoid such situations.

- You may discuss this further with me at any time at (contact information).

- I look forward to hearing from you.

- I have enclosed the checks/emails/photo _____.

- I look forward to your reply and will wait until (the date) before seeking help from a consumer protection agency.

- I believe that this issue will be resolved in due time.

- I hope to restore the trust I have in your company.

- Thank you for your consideration.

Dos and Don'ts of Complaint Letter Writing

If you are still struggling with your letter, here are some tips which might be helpful.

Dos

- Get straight to the point. Write the letter in a concise, factual way.

- Address the letter preferably to the top officer, owner, or director of the company. Your problem will be resolved more quickly and efficiently if you reach someone with authority who is capable of making the decisions.

- Clearly let the company know what exactly you want from them, whether it is just an apology, refund, or replacement of the product.

- Indicate a time frame within which you will be expecting the company's response before turning to the other authorities. Normally two weeks is sufficient time.

- Also, indicate that if the company does not cooperate in good faith, you will seek formal dispute resolution.

- Recap the timeline of the event which has led to your letter of complaint: when you bought the product or used the service, whether you attempted to resolve the issue before, what response you received, and so on.

- Provide all relevant facts and details and try to support them with documents, such as checks, photos, and any other records.

- Keep the letter succinct and short.

Don'ts

- Avoid being rude or sarcastic and do not use any abusive language.

- Stick to the point and avoid criticizing the company in general. You should concentrate on the particular issue which prompted you to write the letter.

- Avoid putting the blame on the person you are addressing. In most cases, they would not be the one who wronged you, so being rude or accusatory to them will not only be discourteous but also unfair.

- Do not allow emotions to overcome you and make sure you have had some time to cool down before writing the letter. Being angry will not make you more persuasive.

Questions and Answers on Complaint Letters

Writing a letter of complaint may be quite a difficult affair, as you are likely already emotionally exhausted because of the issue. Here are answers to some questions you may have before starting to write.

Q: What should I do if the company fails to respond or I am dissatisfied with their response?

A: In this case, file a formal complaint with the customer rights protection agency, the Better Business Bureau, or another similar organization, and do not forget to attach the copy of your initial letter of complaint. All further instructions can be found on the websites of these companies.

Q: Do I have to call or email the company before writing a letter of complaint? Is there any difference?

A: In most cases, companies have a customer service department, which will be your first stop when the issue arises. If they fail to resolve the problem, however, you will write a complaint letter, which becomes a piece of formal documentation, and is addressed no longer to the customer service but the figure of authority. In the case of any further formal or legal proceedings, this letter will be used to support your position. If you have complained previously verbally or by email, mention this fact in your letter.

Works Cited

Better Business Bureau. "Writing an Effective Complaint Letter." *Bbb*,

    https://www.bbb.org/washington-dc-eastern-pa/get-consumer-help/complaints/writing-an-

    effective-complaint-letter/. Accessed 26 July 2017.

Citizens Advice. "Complaint About a Problem at Work – Grievance Letter Checklist."

    Citizensadvice, 2017, https://www.citizensadvice.org.uk/work/problems-at-work/complaint-

    about-a-problem-at-work-grievance-letter-checklist/. Accessed 26 July 2017.

Federal Trade Commission. "Solving Consumer Problems." *Consumer Information*, 2012,

    https://www.consumer.ftc.gov/articles/0228-solving-consumer-problems. Accessed 26 July

    2017.

"How to Write a Complaint Letter." *Academichelp*, 2013, https://academichelp.net/letter-writing-

    help/write-complaint-letter.html. Accessed 26 July 2017.

"How to Write a Complaint Letter." *Answershark*, 2017, https://answershark.com/writing/business-

    letters/how-to-write-complaint-letter.html. Accessed 26 July 2017.

"Sample Complaint Letter Template." *Usa.gov*, 2017, https://www.usa.gov/complaint-letter.

    Accessed 26 July 2017.

Complaint Letter to Your Local Internet Provider

Dear Sir or Madam,

I am writing to express my deep dissatisfaction with the quality of internet service your company provides, as well as with the effectiveness of your company's support service. I started to use your internet service three weeks ago after I had seen an advertisement that claimed your company could provide a high-speed internet connection in my area. I expected to have a promised high-quality internet connection with an average speed of 10 Mbits/second. However, when the connection was established, the speed of the internet turned out to be no higher than 1 Mbit/second. After a few days of dissatisfying experiences with internet use, I contacted your company's support service and expressed my concern. I was told that it was just a temporary issue and that the signal speed will grow to the promised 64 Mbits/second in a few days.

After another week of no improvements in internet speed, I contacted the support service again to receive an explanation. This time I was told that a service worker would be sent the next day to my house to check the connection and identify the problem. Although the service worker did come the next day, this did not improve the situation. I asked the worker to look whether there were any issues with my computer that caused the low-quality signal. He checked it, told me he made some modifications that should solve the problem and charged me for additional analysis. Despite that, the signal speed did not improve, staying at the same level of 1 Mbit/second. My further calls to the support service of your company did not result in any fruitful cooperation, as they did not know what the problem was with my internet connection and offered once more a service worker's visit.

I have been using your company's internet service for three weeks now. All this time I have been paying for a high-quality internet connection advertised as having an average speed of 64 Mbits/second while being forced to face a rather low speed of 1 Mbit/second. Not only have I been paying for the service that did not reach neither my expectations nor the "Premium" internet package that I ordered, but I have also paid the additional fee for the help of your company's service worker, which did not bring any positive changes. I find this situation frustrating and highly uncomfortable, as I am working from my home and, therefore, my working productivity depends on the speed of internet connection. When I decided to use your internet provider service, I was hoping to increase my working effectiveness. In fact, I am now even less satisfied with the internet speed than I was before using your service. Access to the internet is a highly important need in the modern world, so I cannot continue to endure such inconveniences.

I would like you to take every possible action to resolve my issue of low-quality speed connection. If you don't, I will have no other choice than to just switch to the service of another internet provider. I am willing to cooperate and provide any important information that might be helpful in resolving the issue. I hope this problem will be solved as soon as possible and I will happily continue to use your company's internet service. Thank you for your assistance.

Sincerely,

John Colbert

Complaint Letter – The Delivery Time of Electronic Goods

Return Address

Jane Rose
652 Meeker Ave, #300
Brooklyn, NY 11222

Recipient's Address

Electronic Goods For You Inc.
74 Guernsey St.
Brooklyn, NY 11222

Dear Sir / Madam,

I am writing this letter to complain about the problems that arose when discussing the delivery time

for my order on June 5, 2017. In the evening of June 4, 2017, in the online store

ElectronicGoodsForYou, I chose and paid for the Bosch electric kettle. The site offered me a form

to fill, in which I had to specify my address to receive the good, and offered to choose one of three

options for the delivery time. The site stated that there are morning hours, daytime or evening

hours. Since I work in the office, the third option was convenient for me. After filling out all the

fields of the questionnaire, I received the email saying that the support will contact me the next

morning to clarify the details and to choose the delivery time more individually.

The next morning I received a call from support service, during which we confirmed the place of

delivery. However, when I said that I expect delivery at 7 p.m., the behavior of the representative

upset me. At first, he stated that it is impossible because the company does not practice late

deliveries in my district. I replied that the site did not inform me about this obstacle, but on the

contrary, offered to choose such delivery hours. The employee rather rudely and impressively replied that he does not know what the site offered me, but my kettle would be delivered between 12 a.m. and 6 p.m. Since I work at this time, I replied that this option does not suit me. Unfortunately, the worker answered that it was not his problem. I refused this proposition, as I cannot miss work.

I hope that the Service Manager will be able to solve this problem and ensure the delivery of my purchase at a time that is convenient for me.

Sincerely,

Customer's Name
Account number

Cover Letter Writing Guide

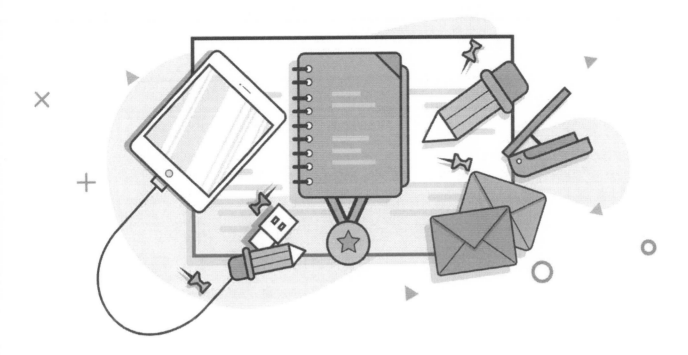

Definition and Aim of a Cover Letter

A cover letter, also called a motivation letter, is a short essay you send with your job application. In it, you provide the additional information about your qualification, discuss any relevant details which may be absent from the CV, and, last but not least, give a glimpse of your personality.

While the major goal of other application documents is to provide factual information about your skills and qualification, in the cover letter you have an opportunity to clarify how exactly those skills may be applied to the position you are after, as well as emphasize your interest in the job. The goal of the cover letter is to demonstrate your interest in the position, clarify why you are suitable for it, as well as demonstrate your knowledge of the company and the job's requirements. The letter explores not only your professional skills and experience but also your personality.

The cover letter is a testimony not only to your skills but also your character, so do not neglect an opportunity to add a bit of a personal touch and warm up the hiring manager. The cover letter would form their first impression of you. Taking into account the fact they are dealing with numerous letters during the hiring process, it is important to do your best to grab their attention and distinguish yourself from your competitors. It is also vital to get rid of any mistakes and typos, as they might kill the chances your CV will even be read.

Even if the company's requirements do not state explicitly that you need to attach a cover letter, you'd better consider writing one: it would show that you put effort into your application.

Steps on How to Write a Cover Letter

Any endeavor becomes less stressful if you divide it into the smaller tasks, which are easier to accomplish. So if the thought of writing a cover letter makes you anxious, here are some simple steps to guide your writing process and help you to overcome the fear of a blank page.

1. Collect information about the potential employer and the position you are applying for. Reread the ad, visit the company's website and make inquiries if you have any acquaintances working for the company. Note its goals and values and think about how you can incorporate them into your application. If possible, you also should find out the name of the person you would be addressing in your letter.

2. Make a list of your skills and qualifications and highlight those you believe to be the most relevant and valuable for the position you are applying for. In the first paragraph, state the reason you are writing, clearly indicating the position and the way you have learned about its opening.

3. List specific reasons why you are suitable for the position, making a connection between your skills and experience and the job's requirements. Use the knowledge you have obtained as proof you have done your research and therefore are genuinely interested in the position.

4. State that you are ready for the interview at the hiring manager's convenience and, if it is not clarified in the ad or job description, indicate when you would be able to start working.

Let the hiring manager know they are free to contact you if they need any further information regarding your application.

5. Check the formatting. The letter would usually be single-spaced. You should also leave a space between each paragraph, greeting included, and three spaces before the signature.

6. Proofread, get rid of any unnecessary details, and make sure your grammar and punctuation are blameless. If there is someone you might ask to have a look at your letter, do it.

7. Don't forget to attach the CV and any other documents you would need to send!

The Structure of a Cover Letter

If you are sending your letter via email, which is the case more often than not, you need to keep in mind some typical elements your letter would consist of.

What to Include in Your Letter

Subject. As the subject of your letter, you may write "Application for the (name of the position) Position."

Greetings. This is the part of the letter you always begin with, as you acknowledge the person you are writing to. It is always preferable to address your respondent by their name, and there is a good chance you would be able to find the name in the job ad or on the company's website. In this case, the ideal ways of addressing will be:

Dear Mr./Mrs. Last Name

If you know your recipient has an academic degree or any other title which would change the mode of address, of course, use those. In case you are not sure of the gender of your recipient, you would write:

Dear First Name Last Name

If you don't know the name, however, you may choose one of the following modes of address:

Dear Sir or Madam

Dear hiring professionals/Dear hiring manager

Dear selection committee

It is better to avoid writing "To Whom It May Concern:" it is too formal and generic and would not endear you to the recipient.

Introduction. In the introductory paragraph, you indicate explicitly for which position you are applying, as well as from where you learned about it. In particular, you should mention if you heard about if from an acquaintance working for the company, its partners or any other contacts associated with the potential employer. Here you may also write why you are interested in the job and briefly give an overview of how your skills and experience match the position. However, do not get into details just yet.

The body of the letter. In two to four paragraphs, you should explain what makes you qualified for the job. The most important thing here is to avoid simply repeating what is already in your CV and instead demonstrate how your skills and experience may be applied to the specific job you want to get. You interpret the facts that are listed in your CV. Think of it as an argumentative essay, where you are trying to provide the strongest evidence to support your claim that your skills match the company's requirements. It is a good idea to either use a bullet list or divide the body of the letter into shorter paragraphs, which would be easier to perceive than the single long one. Try to follow the "show not tell" tip as much as possible: examples and specific cases would be more convincing than simple claims.

Closing. In the closing paragraph, you restate your major point, include your contact information and thank the recipient for their time. Your signature would look like this:

Sincerely/Best regards,

Your Name,

Contact information.

Useful Expressions for Writing a Cover Letter

You would not want your cover letter to consist only of cliches and set expressions. However, there are some which might stir your thought process and save the time you otherwise would have spent agonizing over the appropriate way to express your thoughts.

Introduction

- I am expressing my interest in the position (the name of the position) at (the name of the company) which was advertised in____.

- I am very interested in the position of ____.

- Please find my enclosed CV in the application for the (the name of the position) position advertised in____.

- I saw your advertisement for the vacant position of ____.

- I decided to apply for the vacancy because____.

- I was excited to see your opening for ____.

- I hope to be invited for an interview.

The body of the letter

- I have worked as a ____ for the last ____.

- I am interested in this position because____.

- My experience/skills/qualification prepares me well for ____.

- My work/study was focused on (subject/topic/issue)… which makes me qualified for ____.

- I have a wide range of skills to match the position you describe:

- My background includes____.

- Most recently, I worked (the name of your position) and my responsibilities included ____.

- In the position I previously occupied, I demonstrated the ability to ____.

- During this time, I have (state your accomplishments) ____.

- My knowledge and experience make me qualified for this position because ____.

- I wish to work in a competitive environment and am ready to face new challenges, and therefore I am applying for this position.

Closing

- Please check the accompanying resume for details of my experience and education.

- I am confident that I can offer you the skills you are looking for.

- I am sure I can become a valuable member of your team.

- I look forward to hearing from you.

- I await a response at your earliest convenience.

- Thank you for your time.

- If you have any further questions, please contact me via ____.

- If you require any additional information about me, please contact me via ____.

- I would enjoy working as ____.

Dos and Don'ts of Cover Letter Writing

It would be easier for you to compose an efficient cover letter if you keep in mind these tips and avoid common mistakes.

Dos

- Keep the letter brief. If the company you are applying for has any specific requirements, naturally, follow them, but in most cases, one page is more than enough.

- Feel free to emphasize your skills, experience, and talents, but avoid bragging.

- You might highlight your accomplishments, using a bullet point list. In any case, make sure the recipient would not miss the most significant points, and formatting is your best friend in this endeavor.

- Write the letter from scratch, trying to aim for natural speech. It is not a good idea to copy and paste a ready-made cover letter, regardless whether it was written on your own or, even more so, if it is a template.

- Variegate your sentences' openings. Too much "I" at the beginning looks poor.

- Write consistently. Do not just list your qualities and skills and do not jump from one to another. Make sure to make smooth transitions.

Don'ts

- Do not overindulge in long sentences and passive voice. Your writing should be succinct.

- While highlighting your accomplishments, do not exaggerate or tell outright lies, especially if they are contradicting your CV.

- Avoid including irrelevant information, whether it is about your job experience or your personal life.

- Also, avoid just restating what is already on your CV. Make sure to either provide additional details or put the facts into perspective.

- Do not mention the salary you expect to receive unless it is requested by the company.

- Avoid sounding desperate. Even if this position is your last chance to get a job, there is no need for the hiring manager to know it.

- You should sound neither too persistent nor indifferent. It is good to demonstrate some enthusiasm, but do not throw all your persuasion skills into convincing the manager to hire you.

- Do not get too informal, but try to express yourself with natural language.

Questions and Answers on Cover Letters

Here are answers to the few questions you still might have about cover letters.

Q: Can I get creative with the cover letter or does it have to be a piece of formal writing?

A: That would depend on the nature of the job you are applying for. If the position requires creative skills, you might as well start demonstrating them from the very beginning. It would be especially so if the position has something to do with creative writing. However, in any case, keep in mind the position's requirements: writing a poem if you are applying for an editing job, for example, might be a bit overkill.

Q: What if I am not sending a CV as a response to the open vacancy but want instead to inquire whether there is one?

A: The basics of the cover letter would remain the same. If you are not sure which position might be open, of course, it would be harder to show that you are suitable for it, and it is even more important to do your research carefully and align yourself with the company's specifics and values.

Works Cited

Doyle, Alison. "How to Write a Successful Cover Letter." *The Balance*, 2017,

    https://www.thebalance.com/how-to-write-a-cover-letter-2060169. Accessed 5 July 2017.

"How to Write a Cover Letter." *Academichelp.net*, 2017, https://academichelp.net/business-writing-

    help/employment/write-cover-letter.html. Accessed 6 July 2017.

"How to Write a Cover Letter." *Answershark.com*, 2017, https://answershark.com/writing/business-

    letters/how-to-write-cover-letter.html. Accessed 8 July 2017.

Olson, Angie, and Allen Breeze. "What Is a Cover Letter?" *Owl.English.Purdue.edu*, 2011,

    https://owl.english.purdue.edu/owl/resource/549/1/. Accessed 8 July 2017.

"Purdue OWL: Cover Letter Workshop." *Owl.English.Purdue.edu*,

    https://owl.english.purdue.edu/owl/resource/723/03/. Accessed 7 July 2017.

"Three Excellent Cover Letter Examples." *The Guardian*, 2014,

    https://www.theguardian.com/careers/covering-letter-examples. Accessed 6 July 2017.

Cover Letter for the Position of Middle PHP Coder

Alfred Wayne
Email: aflredwayne@gothamail.com
Mobile: XXX XXXX XXXX

Mr. Joseph J. Kerr

Future Dev and Innovations Inc.

Phone: XX XXXX XXXX

Email: hr.department@fdi.com

RE: Application for Middle PHP coder

Dear Mr. Kerr,

I am writing to you to apply for a Middle PHP coder position, as I saw it in the advertisement on

stackoverflow.com. The features that might make my candidature fitting for your needs:

- 10 years of involvement in the programming field.

- 2 years of working as a PHP Junior in a small organization.

- 1.5 years of in-house work break and freelancing at that time.

My qualities are a love for programming, creativity, and devotion to the cause. I have been attracted

to PHP when I saw the possibilities of server-client interactions the language allows and the

simplicity of implementing it. After 6.5 years of programming at the University and at home during

my free time (C, C++, C#, Java, Python, Delphi), I have decided to deepen my knowledge in PHP.

Working in a small organization gave me the basic understanding of a programmer working process

as well as the skill to learn large amounts of information quickly and efficiently.

However, the job has limited my capabilities, and the work was dull and monotonic, and I decided to leave it and started freelancing. Also, I have damaged my legs in an accident and had to be put in a wheelchair for 1.5 years. Freelancing was an interesting experience that allowed me to choose what I want to create, which has greatly expanded my skills in making computer graphics using databases in unusual manners, and coding a server and a client side of a simple online game. During the freelancing time, I have been coding from home, and have gathered 15 works that showcase my experience and are worth mentioning while applying for the vacancy. You can check them at my personal website: www.alfredwaynedev.com.

Both small company and freelance experiences have brought me a certain set of skills and qualities, but now I have to move forward, and I see the job at Future Dev and Innovations Inc. as the proper next step in my career. The description of the vacancy at your website states that the workers have a decent amount of freedom of self-expression and very interesting projects and tasks. If the information is true, I am very interested in applying for it and getting the job. I will greatly appreciate if you look over my PHP skills and the set of related skills in the resume. If you find my candidature appropriate, I will gladly agree to meet you personally and discuss all the aspects of the job.

I realize that the level of FDI is very high and hundreds of professionals work there, so if my portfolio is not enough for evaluating my skills, you could give me a test task, and I will gladly complete it for you. If the portfolio is enough for your evaluation process, please contact me via email or mobile phone. I am available every day from 7 AM to 9 PM. I am very happy to be acknowledged about the opportunities you offer, and I appreciate your time very much. I hope we will have a great and productive time working together.

Sincerely,

Alfred Wayne

Cover Letter for the Position of In-House Editor

Return Address

Anna Black
103 B Circle Ave, #115
Boston, VA 20094

Recipient's Address

Jeremy Brown
Fashion-Scout Magazine
300 NE 2nd Ave
Miami, FL 42567

Dear Mr. Brown!

I am highly interested in your open position of in-house editor and would like to apply for this vacancy. My experience includes deep knowledge in the sphere of journalism as well as excellent skills in creative writing and editing. Also, I am a rabid reader of your online magazine. I am ready to learn new things as well as to accept criticism and improve my skills. I am also communicative, social, and creative.

My experience includes high education in journalism, and I have also finished the online course of PR. I have also worked as a writer in the "Today" magazine, where I was leading a humorous column. You may wonder why having worked as a writer, I would want to change my field of occupation. Firstly, it may be difficult to write exactly what the reader wants to receive. Having worked in this position for two years, I have realized that readers may not have enough interest in reading anecdotes and funny stories. People differ and each of us accepts humor differently. Secondly, I believe that I can provide your magazine with a high-quality work, and I can guide writers, correct their mistakes, and organize the article in such a way that it would call interest to the quality of the content.

I am particularly inspired by getting a job in your online magazine as it specializes in fashion. I have taken a course of fashion journalism in the university, and I have also visited many fashion events, including Fashion Weeks in many countries. I personally try to follow the tendencies in this industry, so I cannot say that your specialization is new for me. When I visited events devoted to fashion, I used to leave feedback in my social networks, which gathered many comments and much appreciation. So if you become interested in them, I can provide you with some examples.

My experience also includes working as a private teacher for two months while I was a student, so I know how to check various compositions, and how to be unbiased while working with others writing.

Once I traveled to Paris to get to a Fashion Week. I visited it, wrote feedback and posted it on Facebook. I was contacted by a young talented designer, who took notice of my postings. She suggested me to write posts about her collections and manage a blog from her name. We had to stop cooperation as she decided to continue this job by her own, as she finished working on her collection and had enough time for it. Besides, she has received a huge audience, and she wanted to communicate with them because she considered me writing for her as cheating. I was suggested to work as an assistant, helping to answer emails or phone calls, but this was not enough for me.

Now am working as a PR specialist for an IT company, but feel that I should pursue the field to which I am best acclimated. Despite the fact that I perform well and have career opportunities, I am ready to leave this job to work in your journal. I am fascinated by your writers, and I frequently read articles on your website. I would greatly appreciate your acceptance of my candidature. You can contact me by phone or by email at any time. You can find additional information about me on

my resume. I hope to receive a reply from you soon. Thank you!

Best regards,

Anna Black

Follow-Up Letter Writing Guide

Definition and Aim of a Follow-Up Letter

A follow-up letter is a formal letter you send as a follow-up to previous communication with your respondent, whether it was an application letter or resume you have sent, or a job interview. This kind of letter is used to enhance the effectiveness of the previous communication, reinstate the vital points, or remind someone about yourself.

In the business and academic setting, there are various occasions when sending a follow-up letter would be in order. Consequently, the content of the letters would vary according to the particular situation.

In the case of a job application, many applicants avoid writing follow-ups, as they do not want to bother the hiring manager. This approach, however, is wrong. The follow-up is a vital part of the selection process and can boost your position, especially if assertiveness and soft skills are among the qualities necessary for the job you are applying for.

You will write a follow-up letter on the following occasions:

- **No response follow-up.** You have sent a cover letter with resume or a CV to the potential employer, but you have not heard from them since then.

- **Follow-up thank you.** After the job interview, you write the letter of acknowledgment to your potential employer, confirming your interest in the position and providing, if necessary, any additional information.

- **Follow-up to renew the contract.**

- **Reminder follow-up.** After an interview, meeting or a phone call, it might be necessary to summarize the discussed points and remind the participants what was decided.

The first two types of the follow-up letters are the most common. They follow a typical formal structure, so you might want to create a template which you would be able to adjust according to the particular situations and respondents.

The follow-up letter is another chance to attract attention and show yourself in the best light possible. You will want to emphasize your interest and be seen as determined, courteous, and assertive, but not obtrusive or too pushy. Finding the middle ground between excessive politeness and pushiness might be tricky, but it would pay off.

Steps on How to Write a Follow-Up Letter

No Response Follow-Up

Your major goal here is to check whether the employer has received your application and to emphasize that you are still interested in the position. You would want to follow these steps:

1. Make up a list of all necessary information. Look up the date of your previous letter or interview.

2. State the reason why are you writing. Reference your first letter so that the respondent can find it.

3. Ask whether the employer or hiring manager have received your letter. It might have been lost in the junk mail.

4. Next, if the employer has received the documents, you may ask whether they were able to find the time to review them and whether they are considering inviting you for the interview.

5. If the letter was not received, offer to resend it and check twice the email address. If it is possible, you may also consider offering to visit the office and drop off the documents in person.

Thank You Follow-Up After the Job Interview

In this type of letter, your goal is to show the appreciation for the hiring manager's efforts and to reinstate your interest in the position. Here is a list of the things you might want to take into account while writing:

1. First of all, thank the employer or hiring manager for the interview.

2. Next, you might provide a brief summary of your interview or any other previous communications so that the employer recalls you. You should also mention the date of the interview for this purpose.

3. You might include an analysis of the interview. If you have learned something new about the company or if something has especially impressed you, it is worth mentioning.

4. Reiterate the reasons why you think you are qualified for the job. If you have forgotten to mention some relevant information about your experience or qualification, it is time to do it.

5. Don't forget to proofread the letter!

The Structure of a Follow-Up Letter

What to Include in Your Letter

Assuming you would be sending your letter via email, the typical elements of your follow-up would be the following.

Subject. You may indicate the subject of the letter as "Following up on (your position) application/interview." You might also want to indicate the date of your first letter or the interview.

Greetings. This is the part of the letter you always begin with, as you address and acknowledge the person you are writing to. It is always preferable to address your respondent by their name, and it generally should be possible as you have communicated with them earlier. If you are not sure, you may want to check the job ad for the contact person, look up the company's website, or call the company.

So, the ideal ways of addressing the recipient will be:

Dear Mr./Mrs. Last Name

　　　　or

Dear First Name Last Name

The latter is especially useful when you don't know the gender of your respondent. If you know your respondent has an academic degree, of course, you include it in your address. If you don't know the name, you may choose one of the following modes of address:

Dear Sir or Madam

Dear hiring professionals

Dear selection committee

Dear hiring manager

The body of the letter:

• In the opening paragraph, you state the reason for writing and indicate the date of the previous letter/interview. If that's an interview follow-up, you also thank for the interview here.

• In the second paragraph, you either question whether the letter was received and reviewed or provide a summary and/or analysis of the interview.

• The third paragraph is reserved for the interview follow-ups, and here you can remind the interviewer why you are suitable for the job.

• In any case, you would want to be succinct!

Closing. Closing is the last part of the letter where you make your farewells. It would usually look like this:

Sincerely/Best regards,

Your Name,

Contact information (optional).

Useful Expressions for Writing a Follow-Up Letter

There are phrases which are commonplace in this type of letter and which might make composing follow-ups easier for you. Here is a general list categorized by introduction, body, and conclusion.

Introduction

- I am writing regarding the letter/interview on (date).

- I was wondering whether you received and/or had time to review the letter/application/CV I sent you on (date).

- In reference to my email of (date).

- I am following up to make sure/inquire whether you received the letter/documents I sent (date).

Body paragraph

- I am looking forward to meeting with you to discuss the _____ position.

- I believe my qualification/experience will allow me to be a valuable member of your team.

- It was a pleasure meeting you and learning more about the _____ position or/and the company.

- I would be happy to provide any further information.

Closing

- I await a response at your earliest convenience.

- Look forward to hearing from you.

- Thank you for your time.

- Thank you for taking the time to interview me for the _____ position.

- If you have any further questions, please contact me at (email or phone number).

Dos and Don'ts of Follow-Up Letter Writing

There are some tips you should take into account while writing a follow-up letter. Here is a list of the things you should keep in mind and the mistakes you'd better avoid.

Dos

- If it is a no response follow-up, you normally write after 10-14 days after sending your resume.

- If it is a follow-up after a job interview, the ideal time would be within 24 hours after the interview, when the interviewer's memory of you is still fresh.

- In any case, indicate the date of your first communication.

- It is preferable to address your respondent by their name. If you are not sure, you might want to look up the company's website or the job ad.

- Take a proactive position, because in many cases follow-ups are a significant part of the hiring process.

- Be as specific as possible.

- Follow the format and style standard for business letters.

Don'ts

- Do not repeat what you have already written. If you want to remind your respondent about the interview, be brief. Do not give too much information.

- Avoid clichéd phrases and generalizations while describing your impressions of the company or discussing the interview. Writing "it was very interesting, and I have learned much" is not an option.

Questions and Answers on Follow-Up Letters

Follow-up letters might not be something you write or receive every day. So if you are still a bit confused, here are some common questions that might occur and the answers to them.

Q: When should I write a no response follow-up letter?

A: If you haven't heard from the employer ten days after you have sent a resume/application letter, it is perfectly acceptable to remind them of your previous correspondence. Be patient, as they are most likely busy, but you would not want to lose a chance to get this job simply because your letter got lost in the junk mail and you were too shy to check.

Q: Why should I write a follow-up letter after an interview?

A: This way, you show the appreciation for the efforts of the interviewer and reinstate your interest in the position. In fact, some companies take follow-ups into account as a vital part of the hiring process, so you might increase your chances at getting the job you want.

Q: What should my letter look like?

A: You would want to use simple, readable fonts, such as Times New Roman or Arial, with 10-12 point font size, and single-space the letter. You might wish to use the same font you used in your resume or cover letter. You may choose to format in block style, with no indents and with all lines aligned to the left, which is the most common style for business letters. However, modified block (the body text is left justified, and the date and closing are tabbed to the center) and semi-block are also acceptable. In any case, you should follow a consistent formatting style throughout your correspondence.

Works Cited

Brizee, Allen. "Follow-Up & Thank You Letter Overview." *Purdue OWL Engagement*, 2009,

https://owl.english.purdue.edu/engagement/34/43/135/. Accessed 21 July 2017.

"Follow-Up to an Interview." *Purdue OWL*, 2010,

https://owl.english.purdue.edu/owl/resource/634/03/. Accessed 20 July 2017.

"How to Write a Business Letter." *Academichelp.net*, 2012, https://academichelp.net/business-

writing-help/write-business-letter.html. Accessed 19 July 2017.

"How to Write a Follow-Up Letter." *Answershark.com*, 2017,

https://answershark.com/writing/business-letters/how-to-write-follow-up-letter.html.

Accessed 19 July 2017.

Mendlin, Ronald C. et al. *Job Search Tools*. 1st ed., Indianapolis, IN, JIST, 2000.

Follow-Up Letter to a Client

Return Address

Jonathan Willson
123 6th St, #213
Melbourne, FL 32904

Recipient's Address

Frank Rogers
Officeline Inc.
123 6th St.
Melbourne, FL 32904

Dear Frank Rogers,

I am writing to you about our agreement for the sale of furniture. Thirty days ago, you called our company and agreed to purchase the following goods: 28 office desks (Ashley), 30 office chairs (Ashley), 1 leather sofa (Royal), and 2 case cabinets (Royal). I would like to remind you that all of the above furniture has been packed for more than three weeks and ready to be shipped. However, I have not received any information on the delivery and financial issues from you, which has an unfavorable effect on the work of our company. I still believe that at the moment you are still interested in buying the furniture. If so, I would like to ask you to respond to this letter or call me using the phone number which I gave you during our previous conversation.

Since a long time has passed from when we agreed on our deal, the furniture suppliers, from whom I pre-ordered the goods for you, are unhappy with the delay in the delivery and informed me of their intention to withdraw the said lot within the next seven days in case of the following uncertainty. I am extremely interested in completing this deal in the nearest possible date, as I do not want to worsen the relations with suppliers which I have been working with for quite some time. Therefore, I would like to discuss all the details of this transaction with you as soon as possible.

In case you have changed the plans for buying our furniture, I would like to assure you that I do not have any claims and if you want to cancel the order, there is nothing to worry about: our company will not provide you with any additional bills for the retention of the order. However, it is necessary to understand that this order must be brought to its logical conclusion and it would be appropriate for you to inform me of your final decision. If you are not satisfied by any conditions of our deal, I will be happy to help you with this. As I said, you can write or call me anytime, and I am ready to discuss with you all the conditions and details and possibly make some changes to our arrangement. I also have to remind you that if you would not contact me about the order within a few days, I will have to cancel it and you will not be able to buy these products. In the light of all the above, I hope that we will be able to find a compromise.

By the way, as far as I understand, you are arranging an office now, you not? If so, then I have a great offer for you. Most recently, we signed a contract with Samsung, which is the undisputed leader in the market. On this, our customers are now available to order electronic equipment, also, because the contract turned out to be very profitable, the prices for the wholesale purchase of electronic equipment are lower than what other companies could offer. If you still would confirm your order for the purchase of furniture, then you will become our client and receive a discount for 10% off on all subsequent purchases, which will almost double your discount for the purchase of hardware and other office equipment. If I were you, I would not miss such an opportunity.

Sincerely,

Jonathan Willson
Tel. 559-382-6391

Follow-Up Letter for the Position of Web Designer

Return Address

Owen Wilson
555 E Lafayette St, #145
Detroit, MI 48226

Recipient's Address

Mr. David White, General Motors HR Manager
PO Box 33170
Detroit, MI 48232-5170

Dear Mr. White,

I would like to express my gratitude to you for maintaining the conversation with me on the web designer position on Thursday morning. I highly appreciate the opportunity to learn more about General Motors and the nuances of the position offered.

During the interview, we discussed the internal environment of the company I am applying for. General Motors is the leading company in the automobile manufacturing industry, which provokes my desire to become a part of this successful team. From my side, I would like to make the contribution to the corporation's performance. I have acquired significant experience in web design, which is one of my initial advantages as an employee. I had been working for Ford Motor Company for six years and have become accustomed to harsh working conditions. In addition, the experience has provided me with the opportunity to be acquainted with particular market changes. I am able to analyze information and convert it for the company into an advantageous web design."

I am eager to get more knowledge and develop my professional qualities. I consider myself as a persistent person who is ready to work for achieving mutual goals. Responsibility and a creative approach to solving tasks are the vital elements during my work performance. I am willing to stay in a competitive environment, as it enhances the possibility to accomplish the top concerns.

I am highly interested in working for General Motors and sharing a workplace with skilled and experienced professionals. Please let me know if you have any questions left.

I look forward to hearing from you.

Sincerely,

Owen Wilson

Final Thoughts

Don't you even dare think we are saying goodbye to you! (Cue the evil laugh!) Okay, never mind — we just always wanted to do this. The truth is that we hope you will find the book useful and refer to it whenever you have difficulties writing a letter.

Business and academic writing is still strictly regulated: remembering and following all those rules can be exhausting. Well, now you don't have to, because you have all the rules, suggestions, and secret tricks collected in one place.

We sincerely hope we helped you to learn how to deliver your thoughts in a clearer way, because clear communication is the path to understanding.